GW00707814

On The Verge

A Farcical Comedy

Peter Horsler

Samuel French—London
New York-Sydney-Toronto-Hollywood

On the Verge

The premiere of this play was given by the Clacton Amateur Dramatic Society at the Westcliff Theatre, under the direction of John Gordon Ash.

Characters –

Bill Flack
Dora Day
Teresa Day, her daughter
Lily Flack, Bill's wife
Gerald Turner
Lionel Flack, Bill's son
Ruth Hill
Debbie Martin
Tom Day
Alison Turner

The action takes place in Bill Flack's cottage, somewhere in the country

ACT I	Scene 1	8 p.m. on a Friday evening in late August
	Scene 2	10 p.m. the same evening
ACT II	Scene 1	11 a.m. Saturday morning
	Scene 2	8 p.m. the same day
	Scene 3	Three hours later

Time—the present

Note On The Set

The play is set on the ground floor of a cottage with a visible bedroom on the first floor (see photograph of set). Although this visible bedroom adds greatly to the play it is not essential to the action and can be dispensed with if staging facilities will not permit its inclusion. Minor amendments have been included in the script to accommodate this change.

The script has been treated throughout (as regards lighting plots, etc.) as though the inset bedroom has been included in the set.

ACT I

SCENE 1

Bill Flack's cottage somewhere in the country. 8 p.m. on a Friday in late August

The cottage is rather dilapidated, and looks as if it has been well lived in. The ground floor is all in one room. To one side is the front door, which opens directly on to an overgrown garden: this can also be seen through a window set above the door. A boarded door at the back of the room opens on to the stairs, which lead up to a visible practical bedroom containing one small single bed. Below the visible bedroom is a recess where a dresser stands. On the other side of the stairs door is a recessed kitchen with a raised floor where there is a stone sink, together with a few shelves and a kitchen range. There is a small window to the side of this kitchen area, and a back door just below the raised area that leads directly to the outside. Below this door is a small Victorian fireplace with a mirror above it. Furniture consists of an old armchair, a large dilapidated sofa and a kitchen table with three chairs set around it

When the Curtain rises, all the cottage doors are open and Bill Flack is peering out of the front door, obviously expecting someone. He turns impatiently and stomps up to shout up the stairs

Flack Dora, what you at, gal? Bin up there hours, you have!

Dora (*off*) Ain't bin more than five minutes, Bill Flack! Lived in this cottage twenty years I has, so what's yer hurry?

Flack You want Lionel ter run yer down the village in the Land Rover don't yer? Well, he ain't got all day. I got work for him ter do.

Dora emerges from the stairs door, carrying two cases and a small parcel

Dora All right, all right, keep yer hair on. (*Shouting back up the stairs*) Teresa, look under the bed, gal, ain't left no shoes have I?

Teresa (*off*) Already done it, Mum, ain't nothing.

Dora If you was half a man, Bill Flack, you'd carry summat, 'stead a letting me lug me arm off.

Flack (*taking the small parcel*) Give it here then, *gal, never asked yer ter move ter no council house, did I?* (*Shoving her towards the back door*) Beats me why yer done it.

Dora Do it now? Well, you try living with no electricity, no water, bloomin' miles from nowhere when you ain't got a car and see how you like it. (*Moving back to shout up the stairs again*) Teresa! (*Turning to Flack again*) 'Nother thing, Bill Flack, you reckon as how you don't have ter pay my Tom more than a boy's wage 'cause he's living in your cottage. (*Shouting and moving above and round the table checking on what is left*) Teresa, come on, gal! What's keeping yer? (*To Flack*) Think he's frit ter move, don't yer?

Flack Give over gabbin', woman, you're worse than my old Lil, you are.

Teresa emerges from the stairs with another case

Teresa (*crossing towards the back door*) Couldn't get it shut no how, rusted up it were.

Dora Now are there anything else I oughter take?

Flack Strike me, woman, had enough time ter think on it ain't yer?

Teresa Got enough ter carry, Mum, ain't we? Uncle Bill said as how dad can borrer the tractor and trailer.

Flack (*going to Dora and moving her towards the back door*) Going are yer, 'cause I ain't waiting no longer?

Dora Don't you shove me, Bill Flack! (*To Teresa*) Reckons as how we're a couple of his old sheep, gal.

Flack ushers Teresa and Dora out

Flack (*shouting after them*) And tell Lionel not ter mess about! Teresa, don't you hang round him, gal, I want him straight back here! (*He slams the door and dashes across to the front door where he stands beckoning to someone off*) Come on, gal! It's past eight already!

Lily Flack enters, red in the face, panting and carrying a pile of sheets and blankets

Lily (*moving to the stairs door*) Doing me best, Bill, ain't I? Near run all the way up from the farm I has; blowed as an old sheep in clover, I are.

The Land Rover starts up and fades away

Got them off then. I don't reckon as how Dora wanted ter go when it come to it.

Flack (*peering out of the front window*) Don't start gabbin' now, woman, you gotter get them beds done!

Lily Doing me best, ain't I? Your fault, you shouldn't have let the cottage by rights when Dora'd paid ter the end of the month.

Flack Thought she was going this morning, didn't I, silly old boot. Fancy moving house at this time.

Lily Wan't ter know you was going ter let it was she?

A car draws up outside

Flack (*pushing Lily up the stairs*) That'll be them. Now see what you've done with yer old yacking. Go on, fix up them beds!

Lily disappears upstairs

Flack closes the stairs door and rushes around, making sure the Days have not left anything

Lily enters the bedroom and starts making the bed

There is a knock on the front door. With a last glance round, Flack goes and opens it

Gerald Turner and Ruth Hill are standing there. She is carrying two suit-cases and Gerald clutches two cardboard boxes to his chest, one holding wine and the other food

Gerald Hello, Mr Flack, you did say about eight, didn't you? May we come in?

Flack Oh-ar, help yerself, Mr Turner.

Gerald enters and moves above the table, where he dumps his boxes. Ruth drops the suitcases just inside the door and follows Gerald across. Flack closes the door

Gerald Oh, Ruth, this is Mr Flack who's rented us the cottage (*To Flack*) I've been telling Miss Hill how much I enjoyed my stay on your farm last summer.

Flack Ooh-ar.

Ruth How do you do.

Gerald Miss Hill is a librarian at the college where I work but this weekend she's acting as my secretary.

Flack (*looking her up and down*) Ooh-ah, secretary is she?

Gerald (*to Ruth*) Well, what do you think?

Ruth (*looking round*) It's not quite ...

Flack Ain't a lot; never said it were much.

Gerald Anyway, it's the genuine thing, eh Ruth? Earthy, lived in.

Flack Lived in all right, still blinking warm.

Gerald Genuine, Ruth, everything's genuine.

Ruth Genuine what?

Gerald Life, rustic life, reeks of it.

Flack (*sniffing*) Don't stink do it? Old Tom's me stockman but he washes regular and Dora wouldn't let him in till he took his boots off.

Ruth Tom? Dora? Is this their cottage then?

Flack Not now, it ain't. Gone and moved to a council house, they has.

Gerald Imagine anyone preferring a council house to this, Ruth.

Ruth Yes, imagine. They've only recently moved then, Mr Flack?

Flack Oh, fair time back now.

Lily disappears into the other bedroom

Gerald Did I meet them when I was here?

Flack Don't suppose yer did, Mr Turner. Dora don't come down the farm all that much and old Tom would've been helping with the harvest when you was here.

Gerald I remember Debbie.

Flack Ooh-ar, you would an' all.

Ruth Who's Debbie?

Flack She helps Tom with the milking and does a bit on the side—for my old woman.

Gerald Delightful child, I expect she's grown a bit since last year.

Flack Ooh-ar, she has an' all. (*Moving to the stairs door, opening it, and showing stairs*) Well, better show yer what's what, ain't I?

Gerald Good idea.

Flack This here's the stairs. They're a bit narrer, all right though if yer don't rush it.

Ruth There are two bedrooms?

Flack (*looking from one to the other*.) Ooh-ar, 'cause you'll want two, won't yer?

Ruth We will, most certainly, Mr Flack.

Gerald Yes, of course, I certainly don't fancy sleeping on that sofa.

Ruth You're sure the beds are aired, Mr Flack?

Flack Aired? I should say they are, just as if they'd bin slept in last night.

Ruth Oh!

Flack All clean clothes though, Mrs is up there putting them on now. (*Opening the stairs door and shouting up the stairs*) You finished them beds yet, Lil?

Lily (*off*) Shan't be two ticks.

Flack (*waving his arm towards the kitchen area*) That there's the kitchen. Still, 'spect you can work it out fer yerselves. No need fer me ter show yer everything, is there?

Gerald No, I'm sure we can manage.

Flack Right, I'll be off then, got plenty ter do. (*Shouting up the stairs*) Lil! (*To Gerald*) You going Sunday night?

Gerald I'm not sure yet.

Ruth I should be in by nine on Monday. It had better be Sunday night.

Flack Well, suit yerselves. Drop the key at the farm when yer ready.

Lily flings open the stairs door, catching Flack with it

What the hell! 'Ang it woman, can't yer look what yer doing! (*He closes the stair door*)

Lily Hello, Mr Turner, I din't know as how it was you he'd let the place to. Close as the grave, he are.

Gerald Ruth, this is Mrs Flack.

Ruth How do you do.

Lily Please ter met yer, I'm sure.

Flack (*opening the door to usher Lily out*) She's his secretary.

Lily That's nice. Staying long then this time, Mr Turner?

Gerald Only the week-end, I'm afraid.

Lily We could put you up at the farm, if you'd rather.

Ruth Oh, well perhaps. . .

Gerald (*quickly*) Very kind, Mrs Flack, but we shall get more work done on our own.

Flack We'll let yer get started then. Come on, Lil. (*He drags her towards the front door*)

Lily Anything you want?

Ruth Some fresh milk and eggs would be nice.

Lily Debbie'll bring yer some if she ain't gone, or I'll send Lionel.

Flack Come on, woman!

Flack pushes Lily ahead of him out of the door

Gerald (*moving to Ruth, spinning her round and embracing her*) Ruth darling, its come true at last.

Flack returns

Flack (*by the open door*) 'Ere, you ain't likely ter light a fire are yer?
Gerald (*breaking from Ruth*) What?
Flack (*pointing to the fireplace*) Only there's an old owl nesting in the stack.
Ruth Owl?
Flack Won't hurt yer, miss.
Gerald Of course not. Well, thank you, Mr Flack.
Flack Thought I'd better warn yer like, case yer smoked yerself out.
Gerald I think we'll be warm enough without fires, don't you, Miss Hill?
Flack Ooh-ar, happen yer will. I'll be off then.

Flack exits closing the door

Gerald Now let's dig ourselves in and forget the outside world.
Ruth (*sitting in the armchair*) Trust an archaeologist to talk of digging in.
Gerald (*unpacking the food box and taking out two plates, two wine glasses, two table napkins, two soup bowls and two sets of knives and forks*) Right, darling, now we'll make everything cosy and ...
Ruth (*heaving herself out of the chair*) You'll have a job to make this chair cosy.
Gerald We shan't need that. Try the sofa. Then, when we've got supper ...
Ruth (*sitting on the sofa and placing her shoulder bag beside her*) Supper? You promised a cooked dinner.
Gerald I was just being modest, modest little Gerald, that's me. While it's cooking, we'll go for a little stroll—good for the appetite.

There is a bellow of a bull from the garden

Ruth (*jumping to her feet and running to the fireplace*) Oh, what on earth!
Gerald Hell! Sounded like the minotaur. (*Dashing up to the kitchen window*) I'll have a look.
Ruth It's not loose, is it?
Gerald Can't see anything.
Flack (*off, as if from the garden outside the back door*) Woe, you old bugger you, I'll belt yer nose if I catch yer!

There is another bellow further off

(*Off*) Don't just stand there, Lil, grab his ring!
Gerald (*rushing to the front window*) They're round this side.
Ruth (*pressing herself to the fireplace*) It can't get in here, can it?
Gerald It's only a cow that's broken loose. Oh, hell, old Flack's coming back here. (*He moves to the front door and opens it.*)

Flack falls in

Flack Ah-oop!
Gerald Sorry, thought I'd save you the trouble of knocking.
Flack Knocking? Oh-ar. Thought I'd better come back and warn yer.
Ruth Warn us, oh!

Gerald About a loose cow.

Flack Bull.

Gerald }
Ruth } Bull! { *Speaking together*

Flack Can't keep the old sod in no-how.

Gerald You never mentioned a bull when I paid you.

Flack I don't charge for him.

Ruth Does he charge us, that's more to the point.

Flack (*breaking into a slow laugh*) Do he charge yer? That's a good un that is—Hamish charge?

Gerald Hamish?

Flack That's his name. Scottish, Aberdeen Angus, see?

Gerald No.

Flack Gentle as a lamb he are, only I thought I'd better warn yer, he don't like being trod on.

Ruth Trod on! What is he, a midget?

Flack In the dark I mean, if yer goes out.

Ruth (*going to stairs door and disappearing up the stairs*) Don't worry, Mr Flack, nothing will induce me to go outside after sunset.

Ruth goes

Flack (*to Gerald*) Thought as how I'd better let yer know like. Can't have no accidents to me guests can I?

Gerald (*aware that Ruth has gone upstairs, moving pointedly to the front door and inviting Flack to go*) Very thoughtful of you, Mr Flack.

Flack 'Sides, I ain't insured.

Gerald No need to worry about us, I can assure you. We've better things to do than go wandering about in the dark.

Flack Ooh-ar, 'spect you have an' all. Be off then. Pop across ter the farm if there's anything else yer want.

Gerald Nothing but a little peace and quiet, Mr Flack, that's all.

Flack goes out. Gerald closes the door and then rushes up the stairs only to be met by Ruth coming down

Ruth (*pushing past him at the foot of the stairs*) You promised a restful weekend

Gerald (*taking her in his arms and trying to propel her back up the stairs*) But it will be darling, and I hope you haven't forgotten your promise.

Ruth (*pushing him back again*) When the setting's right, I said. (*Moving to the fireplace*) It's a long way off yet.

Gerald (*moving above the table*) It won't be. (*He picks up the food box and goes to the kitchen area, calling to her as he goes*) If you're not too tired, you can lay the table.

Ruth goes to the table, removes the wine box into a chair, and starts to lay the table

(*Emptying the container on the draining-board by the sink*) Do you fancy chops, steak or fish?

Ruth I fancy eating before midnight.

Gerald They're all pre-cooked, darling. We can heat them over a saucepan or in the oven.

Ruth (*pulling out bottle after bottle of wine from the box and placing them on the table*) Were you planning a drunken orgy?

Gerald Not a drunken one, darling, but I thought you'd like some choice. What are we having, meat or fish?

Ruth What's the fish?

Gerald Smoked mackerel, cold salmon or trout cooked.

Ruth The trout would be nice.

Gerald (*picking up a bottle of wine and adopting a foreign accent*) In that case, madam, I recommend this one. (*Reading the label*) Chateauneuf du pape.

Ruth Gorgeous.

Gerald (*putting the bottle on the table*) That's settled then. (*Trying to propel her to the stairs door*) Now come and help me choose a bedroom.

Ruth (*crossing below him back to the table*) I'm laying the table and just remember you're here to study an earthwork.

Gerald I am?

Ruth Part of your thesis, I think you said.

Gerald Yes, well I can do that as well.

Ruth As well as what?

Gerald Having a lovely time with you.

Ruth Upstairs, I suppose, choosing a bedroom.

Gerald Or down here on the sofa.

Ruth No, Gerald, I have not come away on a dirty week-end.

Gerald (*feigning shock, and moving to her*) Darling, now be fair. (*Taking her in his arms*) You know I could never think of you like that. I love you for yourself, only yourself, that lovely little self that sometimes overwhelms me.

Ruth (*coolly disengaging*) You really do love me, do you, Gerald?

Gerald (*wrapping his arms round her*) Overwhelmingly.

Ruth (*pushing him away*) And Alison, do you love her?

Gerald Of course I do, only not in the same way.

Ruth In what way then? (*Pushing him towards the sofa*) Go and sit over there and tell me. (*She moves above the table again and continues laying it*)

Gerald (*sitting on the arm of the sofa*) Well, she's important to me of course. I like her company—I'm used to having her around. She's a marvellous cook and—well, we married so young.

Ruth She spoils you, mothers you, does everything for you.

Gerald No—well in a way, I suppose, but she stifles me, won't respond to my romantic spirit. It's being a nurse—she's too damned efficient.

Ruth So you betray her.

Gerald (*rising and moving to the fireplace*) Betray! That's an ugly word to use.

Ruth It's an ugly act.

Gerald (*turning back to her*) I couldn't betray anyone, least of all Alison.

Ruth (*engaging him*) You don't see bringing me to an out-of-the-way cottage in the country with the intention of having your evil way, a betrayal?

Gerald Evil way! (*Laughing and moving to her*) Aren't we a wee bit out of date? (*Taking her arm, pushing her to the sofa and sitting beside her*) Look, come and sit down. Let's talk this thing out. Now, you'd agree that we're not one person but many; that we have different facets to our personalities?

Ruth Yes.

Gerald That we're different people, depending on whom we're with?

Ruth Mmm.

Gerald Well, to be fully alive we need different company so that every facet is stimulated.

Ruth Yes?

Gerald So, there's a side of me that Alison can't touch, can't respond to.

Ruth And that's where I come in?

Gerald Exactly, so you see I need both of you. Love you in different ways.

Ruth Which particular bit loves me?

Gerald (*putting his arm around her*) Darling, need you ask? The deeply passionate side, the emotional, the romantic ...

Ruth (*removing his arm*) In other words, the dirty old man bit.

Gerald (*jumping up and pretending to be deeply hurt*) Hell! Do you have to be so crude? I thought you cared! (*Marching to the table and starting to pack the things back into the box*) I'll take you home.

Ruth follows him up

I hope you've enjoyed your little game. If you must get pleasure from hurting people, I'm delighted to have made you happy. I'm glad! After all, your happiness is everything to me, everything! Everything!

Ruth (*putting back the articles as he continues to remove them*) I'm sorry, Gerald, I didn't mean it. I don't really think of you like that; it's just the mood I'm in after a hard week and that long drive down. Blame this cottage, old Flack, the owl up the chimney and that bull, Hamish. (*Drawing him away*) Come on, let's stay.

Gerald (*taking her hand*) All right, darling, all right, I understand. I know it isn't quite the romantic setting I promised.

Ruth It doesn't matter, really it doesn't.

Gerald (*breaking away and moving back to the table*) We shall never get supper at this rate and we can't go to bed until we have.

Ruth (*yawning*) I could, this minute.

Gerald (*rushing to her and manœuvering her towards the stairs*) Oh, darling, you make me so happy. We'll eat later.

Ruth (*breaking away from him and moving to the table*) No, we won't; I'm also starving. (*Picking up the chosen bottle of wine and thrusting it at him*) You open that, I'll try laying the table again. (*She carries on laying the table*)

Gerald Right, darling. (*He skips up to the sink in the kitchen area with the bottle*) That's funny!

Ruth (*not looking round*) What is?

Gerald There's no tap.

Ruth Don't be silly, there must be.

Gerald (*looking through the window over the sink*) Yes, there is: it's outside.

Ruth Don't be ridiculous, whoever heard ... (*She stops as a terrible thought strikes her*) If the tap's outside, what about ... (*She looks round the room, then dashes to the stairs door and disappears up the stairs*)

Gerald (*returning from the kitchen area*) Well, it is outside. It's what they call a stand-pipe. (*Realizing that she has gone*) Ruth? Ruth, where ... (*Seeing the stairs door open, he moves rapidly to the foot of the stairs*) Don't come down, I ...

Ruth (*pushing past him at the foot of the stairs*) That's it! (*Moving rapidly to the front door*) That is definitely it!

Gerald (*following her down*) I was only joking.

Ruth There's no loo. Do you realize that?

Gerald Yes there is, silly.

Ruth Where then?

Gerald (*drawing her after him into the kitchen area*) Come here! (*Pointing out of the window above the sink*) There you are.

Ruth You don't mean that little barn?

Gerald That's right—with the nettles round the door.

Ruth (*freeing herself and marching down to the front door*) Nettles! Splendid!

Gerald (*dashing after her*) Hold on, no need to panic.

Ruth (*turning on him*) If you think I'm going out there, every time I want to—with nettles up to my ...

Gerald No, of course not.

Ruth Stumbling over a slobbering bull ...

Gerald There won't be any need, darling, there's bound to be a guzzunder.

Ruth A what?

Gerald A potty that goes under the bed.

Ruth (*turning and picking up the cases*) Thank you very much! Good-bye!

Gerald (*going to her and taking the cases*) No, darling, sorry. We'll manage without.

Ruth (*turning and staring at him*) What?

Gerald I mean, we'll be out all day and there are plenty of pubs.

Ruth I shan't dare drink a thing. (*Looking at the wine on the table*) You can pack that lot away for a start.

Gerald (*putting down the cases*) I know it's all been a bit of a shock. I didn't realize—I only saw the place from the outside. (*Indicating the sofa*) Look, sit down for a moment.

Ruth, rather reluctantly, sits

That's better. (*Moving up to the kitchen area*) I'll get us both a drink.

Ruth (*jumping up*) Drink!

Gerald It's all right.

Ruth sits

Then we'll drive down the village after supper and find a pub. (*He takes out a pocket corkscrew and opens the bottle that he had left in the sink*)

Ruth I'm sorry, Gerald, I'm not staying here, spending pennies in a pub miles away.

Gerald (*returning to the table with the bottle*) My fault, darling, I should have checked the place.

Ruth Let's go back. You can always tell Alison the earthwork wasn't any good.

Gerald (*pouring two glasses of wine*) I'm afraid that would be difficult. You see, I rather built up the jolly old earthworks. Had to or she might have smelt a rat. (*Carrying the two glasses over to her and sitting beside her*) Anyway, you wouldn't send me back to the misery of a weekend on my own, would you? Alison's on duty and there are at least three babies about to be born any minute now. (*He hands her a drink*)

Ruth What on earth made your wife want to be a district nurse? Beats me.

Gerald Me, too, but that's Alison, loves every minute of it. Says she does it to counterbalance my preoccupation with the past and the dead.

Ruth Are you in the habit of going off for lonely week-ends to work on earthworks?

Gerald No, I've only been working on it seriously for about a year. (*Putting his arm round her*) But I've been thinking about having a go for some time now; preparing the ground you might say.

Ruth (*removing his hand*) Very appropriate for an archaeologist.

Gerald Yes, it is, isn't it.

Ruth My flatmate thinks I'm at a librarian's conference.

Gerald Well, won't she expect to hear details?

Ruth I hope not. Lucky for us she's too occupied with her new boy-friend at present.

Gerald (*placing his hand on her knee*) You know, I can't think why I only noticed you at the beginning of term. It's a big library but all the same.

Ruth (*removing his hand*) I only came in April.

Gerald (*returning his hand to her knee*) Ah.

Ruth (*looking at his hand*) I suppose you've tried it on with all the others, those under fifty, that is.

Gerald Is that what you really think of me?

Ruth I'm not sure what I think. (*Removing his hand*) I don't know you very well yet, do I? I'm only going by what the juniors told me.

Gerald And what was that?

Ruth "If old Turner's about, watch it," they said, "don't put anything on the bottom shelf; don't be caught bending."

Gerald (*putting his arm round her*) You're an incorrigible liar: they'd never refer to me as old.

Ruth Mind my drink!

Gerald (*taking her glass and placing both glasses on the table*) All right, I confess. Only they didn't tell you everything; they forgot to mention one important fact. (*Diving over the end of the sofa and pinning her beneath him*) I'm an incurable sex maniac!

Ruth Ouch! Stop it, Gerald, you're hurting!

Gerald I've not started yet. Gr-rr-rr.

The front door opens and Debbie, who is nine months pregnant, enters carrying a basket containing milk and eggs

Debbie (*calling as she closes the door*) Anyone about, brought yer milk and eggs. (*Moving in*) Oh, sorry, Dora never answered no doors and I . . . (*She recognizes Gerald*) Uncle "G"! Well I never! Didn't know as it was you what'd got the cottage.

Gerald Debbie!

Ruth (*pushing Gerald off her and sitting bolt upright*) Uncle "G"?

Gerald Well, well, Debbie, how nice to see you. (*Forcing a laugh*) You've caught me at an awkward moment: I was just giving Miss Hill some dictation when I fell over the end of the sofa.

Debbie (*giggling*) Ooh—and she lost her notebook?

Gerald What?

Debbie And her pencil?

Gerald (*kneeling and pretending to search*) Ah, thank you Debbie—must be here somewhere.

Ruth Uncle "G", why don't you stop this charade and introduce me.

Gerald (*getting up sheepishly from his knees*) Ah, yes, well, this is Debbie Martin. She works for Mr Flack; and Debbie, this is Miss Hill who's acting as my secretary for the week-end.

Ruth And perhaps Debbie would like to introduce me to Uncle "G".

Debbie Don't yer know him, then?

Ruth I've not met Uncle "G" yet, no.

Debbie He ain't me uncle really, only called him that 'cause he were so cuddly.

Gerald Looked cuddly, you mean, Debbie, looked cuddly.

Debbie giggles

Ruth It appears that Uncle "G"'s soon to have a nephew or niece or a something?

Gerald I didn't know you were married, Debbie.

Debbie Oh, I ain't married yet.

Ruth Well you don't want to rush these things.

Gerald (*sternly*) I hope you're not mixed up with a married man, Debbie.

Debbie I ain't saying nothing. (*Turning and putting the basket on the table*) If he wants me he'll ask, won't he.

Ruth (*looking at Gerald*) He may not be in a position to ask.

Debbie (*looking at Gerald*) Anyhow, I don't want him, if he don't want me. Well, yer'll be all right for milk and eggs now, won't yer. (*Moving to the front door*) Mrs Flack says I gotta start having early nights, 'case I gets meself inter trouble. (*Putting her head back round the door*) Oh, and she says, if yer hear scratchings in the roof, it'll be the sparrers 'cause old Bill's done in all the rats.

Ruth (*jumping up*) Rats!

Gerald Rats! In the house?

Debbie No, not in the house. Might be a few in the privy though. Never seen nothing but a few old bats in here since he done it. See yer then, Uncle "G". (*As she goes*) Ooh, what a surprise!

Debbie goes out

Ruth (*collecting her bag and crossing to the front door*) Owls, rats, bull, bats! I'm not staying!

Gerald Now, Ruth, don't get into a state over nothing.

Ruth Nothing! You call being incarcerated with a dirty old man in a cottage full of rodents, nothing!

Gerald Dirty old man, I resent that.

Ruth So must Debbie.

Gerald (*moving swiftly to her*) Debbie! Good God, you don't think?

Ruth You stayed at the farm, said so yourself. Keep away from me!

Gerald Not till I've knocked some sense into you. (*Swinging her past him*) Now, just you listen! Yes, I stayed at the farm but over a year ago and as for Debbie, I'm old enough to be ...

Ruth Daddy, yes quite.

Gerald (*picking up the cases*) I'd better put these back in the car then if you really think ... How could you, Ruth? It's as well you'll never know how much you've hurt me.

Ruth All right, Gerald, I'm sorry, it was her calling you Uncle "G". Of course I don't really think ... It's this wretched place—peace and quiet you said, a little rural haven.

Gerald Look, tell you what, let's eat out at the - what was it - the *Red Lion*.

Ruth (*dropping her bag on the sofa*) I shall never be able to sleep here, I know.

Gerald Come now, I'm not that much of a beast.

Ruth (*laughing*) Not that young either.

Gerald Enough of that. (*Indicating the food on the table*) You put this stuff in the kitchen, while I take these cases upstairs. (*He mounts the stairs to the exposed bedroom*) I'll just make sure the bed's all right while I'm up there.

Ruth (*going to the table and packing up the picnic things*) You make sure both beds are all right. I'm not sure of your part of the bargain yet—rural paradise!

Gerald (*off, or from the exposed bedroom*) You'll see: the tranquillity, the country smells, the chatter of little birds ... (*He places Ruth's case under the bed*)

Gerald exits

Ruth (*alone*) The scrabbling of rats, the whirring of bats, the roar of a dirty, great bull. (*She takes the basket that Debbie brought and the picnic box up to the kitchen area*) Not to mention Uncle "G". (*She packs the box and basket out of sight into a cupboard*)

Gerald enters down the stairs

Gerald There, all neatly stowed away under the bed.

Ruth Where have you put my case? Not under the same bed as yours, I hope.

Gerald (*with mock shock*) Don't be disgusting, as if I would leave your case alone with mine without a chaperone.

Ruth (*moving down to mirror to tidy her hair*) Where is it then?

Gerald Under the other bed.

Ruth (*picking up her bag from the sofa*) Good, I don't want to be taken for granted.

Gerald (*moving swiftly to her and embracing her*) Of course not, darling, just taken. Hmm?

Ruth (*disengaging firmly, then taking his arm*) Come along. Is the *Red Lion* another paradise?

Gerald (*walking with her to the front door and opening it*) It's a three-star inn.

Ruth You sure they were stars and not sparrow droppings? (*Breaking away from him as they reach the door*) Oh, what about that damned bull?

Gerald We're not taking him.

Ruth Check he's not outside, idiot! (*She pushes him out*)

Gerald (*returning quickly*) No, there's an anaconda, a few rattlesnakes, a giant rat or two but no bull.

Ruth (*trying to push him out*) Well, go on, Lord of the jungle.

Gerald Jane stay close Tarzan, beasts no come near.

Ruth (*as they go*) Jane more frightened of Tarzan coming too near.

Ruth and Gerald go out. As their laughter dies away, the back door opens and Dora and Teresa enter, followed by Lionel carrying their two cases

Dora (*moving above the table*) Council workmen! Like ter put me boot behind them, I would. Been sick, gal, if I'd stayed there with all that old wet paint. (*She becomes aware of the bottles of wine on the table*) Hello, what's all this here then?

Teresa (*following her, picking up the box of wine from the chair and sitting*) Ooh-er.

Lionel (*not looking in the direction of the table*) Where do yer want these then? Like ter know what cheeky devil parked his old car in the gateway. No flippin' joke carrying these up from the road. (*To Teresa*) What yer gawkin' at, gal?

Teresa This here drink. What's it doin' here?

Dora If old Bill Flack's done it ter keep my Tom from goin' arter another job, he's bin wasting his time, I can tell yer.

Lionel Ain't like dad, he wouldn't give yer nothing.

Dora Must have bin him though; nobody else ain't got a key. (*Packing the bottles back into the box*) Well, he needn't think I'm a going ter drink it.

Lionel Bet he got it as a job lot down the market.

Gerald's car starts up and drives away

(*Racing across to peer out of the front window, still carrying the cases*) There he goes. Wanted ter tell him off, I did. Bloomin' cheek!

Teresa Might have been bigger than you, Lionel.

Lionel (*lifting the cases above his head*) Had to a bin a ruddy giant, gal, afore he'd a frit me.

Dora You can carry those cases up afore you goes then, Lionel, being as you're so strong like.

Lionel moves up to the stairs door

We ain't sleeping with no wet paint. We'll have another night here, gal.

Lionel Where do yer want them then?

Teresa Mine's the rusted one, stick it on me bed.

Lionel goes up the stairs

Dora (*as he goes*) Put them both on the floor, Lionel. We gotta make the beds first. Good job, gal, we left them sheets and blankets in the old cupboard else we'd have had ter carted some back with us.

Lionel appears in the exposed bedroom. He puts down one of the cases and disappears from sight

Teresa (*moving to the fireplace and quizzing herself in the mirror*) Ain't we going ter have summat ter eat afore we goes?

Dora You can if yer like, I ain't getting nothing. I'm off ter roost, I are.

Teresa (*fluffing her hair, etc.*) Good job we met Dad on the way back, else he'd a gone to our new house arter the cricket match.

Dora State he gets in, gal, when he's cricketing, he wouldn't have noticed we wasn't there. Ah, now I sees how old Flack knew we was a coming back: course, yer dad must have told him. Crafty old fox he are. Well, he can have it all back termorrer, I ain't a touching it.

Lionel returns from the bedroom

You get off home now, Lionel. Thank yer for running us down.

Teresa Oh, Mum, can't he stay while I'm having summat ter eat?

Dora (*moving to the stairs door*) Two minutes then, no more, else yer get up ter something you didn't oughter.

Teresa Mum, you ain't got no trust in me, have yer?

Dora (*looking pointedly at Lionel*) Ain't just you gal. Two minutes, mind.

Dora goes up the stairs

Lionel creeps across and closes the stairs door and then vaults over the sofa to grab Teresa. She dodges his embrace and sits on the sofa

Teresa Give over, Lionel, she'll hear us. Anyhow, I'm hungry.

Lionel (*circling round the sofa*) Know what yer hungry for, gal, I do.

Teresa (*giggling*) All you think of, Lionel Flack. Worse than old Hamish you are.

Lionel (*jerking her to her feet*) Can't hang about, gal, only got two minutes! (*He bends her across his knee and kisses her*)

Teresa (*coming up for air*) Oh, Lionel, yer do kiss lovely.

Lionel throws her on the sofa, where she lands with a crash

Dora (*off*) Teresa!

Teresa (*shouting up to Dora*) Shan't be a minute, Mum!

Dora (*off*) Has Lionel gone?

Teresa Just going, Mum.

Lionel charges across and dives on top of her

Dora (*off*) Lily's made the beds up for us so you can come straight up. Teresa!

Teresa (*pushing Lionel off and scrabbling to her feet, straightening her dress, etc*) Just finished me supper, Mum. Ooh, you got me all of a doo-dah, you have, Lionel. You can't go home now.

Lionel (*leaning forward and pinching her seat*) Two minutes ain't no good to a man like me.

Teresa shrieks as he pinches her

Dora (*off*) That Lionel still there! What's he up to?

Lionel jumps to his feet and whispers in Teresa's ear

(*off*) Teresa!

Teresa All right, then, cheeky devil. (*shouting*) Lionel's had a bite, Mum, going now. (*Pushing him across to the front door*) Go on, then!

Lionel (*stomping heavily to the front door and opening it*) Night, then, Teresa. (*He slams the door, but stays*)

Teresa (*in a loud voice as she moves to the stairs door*) Night, Lionel.

Teresa goes up the stairs into the visible bedroom singing a pop song, and we see her strip down to bra and panties. Lionel tiptoes to the sofa·and pulls off his wellingtons

Dora (*off, as Teresa strips and sings*) Enough of that, gel. You get ter bed!

Teresa Right Mum.

Lionel tiptoes to the stairs door and pulls it open

A grim-faced Dora is revealed, with arms folded

Lionel (*backing towards the back door, holding up his wellingtons for her to see*) Little stone, in me wellies.

Lionel turns and dashes out

Dora marches back upstairs into Teresa's room, grabs her by the hair and drags her off. Teresa's song trails off as she does so, and—

the CURTAIN falls

Additional script if the inset bedroom is not used

Teresa (*in a loud voice, as she moves to the stairs door*) 'Night, Lionel. (*To him in a stage whisper.*) Be ready in a minute.

Dora (*as she goes up the stairs after Lionel's exit.*) Right, my gal, you're coming in with me. That'll stop yer hanky panky.

SCENE 2

The same. 10 p.m. the same evening

The curtain rises on an empty set lit by the remaining daylight. Immediately, a car draws up outside and headlights flash across the window. The car doors bang

Ruth (*off*) I swear that's Hamish under those laurels.

Gerald (*off*) He gets about then, you've seen him a dozen times tonight at least.

Ruth and Gerald enter by the front door, both a little giggly from their visit to the pub

Ruth (*as she enters*) Can't get it out of my mind that he's out there somewhere.

Gerald (*moving to her and putting his arms round her*) He's made you cling close to me. Got him to thank for that. (*He goes to the door and puts his head out*) Hamish, Hamish, Hamish! Come along, boy, "G" wants to give you a big thank-you kiss.

A distant bull roar: Gerald jumps back into the room

Ruth Please close that door, Gerald, you're making yourself nervous.

Gerald slams the door

Gerald (*moving to her and putting his arm round her*) Stay close to me, darling, and you haven't a thing to worry about.

Ruth (*disengaging*) I'm not so sure about that either.

Gerald (*nipping up to the stairs door and opening it*) Well, we might as well get an early start.

Ruth What!

Gerald In the morning, make an early start on the earthwork.

Ruth (*moving swiftly up to mount the stairs*) Oh, right, good idea. (*Turning and pushing Gerald back into the room*) No, not yet, not just yet, Gerald, I want to talk to you first.

Gerald (*trying to steer her back to the stairs*) What about? We've done all the talking; it's action time now.

Ruth (*closing the stairs door firmly*) No, we haven't. Besides I'm not going to bed until I'm sure that I won't need to ...

Gerald You can always wake me. I'll escort you madam, through the perils of the nettles, fending off the rampaging Hamish.

Ruth Look, put the light on and come and sit down for a moment. (*She sits on the sofa, putting her handbag down beside the arm*)

Gerald (*going up to the kitchen area*) I suppose there's one somewhere. I didn't think to ask, it being summer.

Ruth A one what?

Gerald (*looking in the cupboards*) Light.

Ruth (*standing*) You don't mean there's no electricity either? (*Falling back in her seat*) Some paradise!

Gerald I don't remember reading that they had all mod. cons. in paradise. (*Finding a lamp*) Ah, here we are. (*He carries a small gas lamp triumphantly to the table*) Complete with new canister, too.

Ruth I hope you know what you're doing with that thing?

Gerald Used to use them on field study. (*He examines the lamp*) There should be a lever to lift the glass somewhere. (*He does so*) Ah, that's it. All I want is a match. (*He takes a box from his pocket, which he leaves on the table*) Ten, nine, eight, seven, six five. (*He strikes the match*) We have ignition, four, three, two, one—lift off. (*He picks up the lamp and swings it round at arm's length*) It's looking good, right on course.

Ruth Gerald, when you've finished playing, I want to talk.

Gerald (*putting the lamp down on the table and looking puzzled*) That's funny.

Ruth What is?

Gerald I could have sworn that we unpacked that box of wine before we went out.

Ruth Don't tell me the place is haunted as well.

Gerald (*going to sit beside her, putting his arms round her*) I must have been wrong, that's all. You're befuddling my senses, clouding my reason, warping my judgement.

Ruth (*removing his arm*) That's precisely what I am doing. I'm sure you'll regret this when you stop to think.

Gerald Yes, I do. I should have insisted that we went straight to bed. Not given way to your whim for a little talk. You're coming over all moral again. (*Putting his arm round her*) Anyway, thinking is counter-productive in matters of the heart.

Ruth (*removing his arm, rising and moving to the table*) I'm talking about you and Alison. Things will never be the same again if you betray her. Don't imagine you can be unfaithful and not suffer regrets. (*Relaxing against the table*) These taboos are generations deep, they can't be disregarded by rationality. You may think you can have a bit on the side ...

Gerald Ruth!

Ruth Well, that's what I am.

Gerald I'd never think of you as that—you know how I feel.

Ruth At the moment, yes. But afterwards ...

Gerald Still the same. I told you, you complement Alison.

Ruth (*moving to sofa and flicking his head*) The theory's fine but you must admit some guilt. Go on, admit it.

Gerald Why should I, she doesn't feel guilty about me.

Ruth (*moving to the fireplace*) She would never be unfaithful to you. She couldn't.

Gerald How would you know? You've never met her.

Ruth (*turning to him*) Well, no, but from what you've said.

Gerald She wouldn't hop into bed with another man, if that's what you mean.

Ruth Well, what other way?

Gerald (*rising and going up to the kitchen area to collect two wine glasses*) All right, if we're going to be serious, I'm having another drink. You going to join me or are you scared of the consequences? (*He goes to the table and pours two drinks*)

Ruth (*sitting on the sofa*) If you think it will help, but don't try to put me off. We've got to have this thing out.

Gerald I wasn't trying to. (*He picks up the two drinks, gives one to Ruth and then sits on a chair at the table*) Here's to the bloody inquisition.

Ruth Well what other way can Alison be unfaithful?

Gerald How could you understand?

Ruth I'll try.

Gerald (*tossing back his drink*) No, I can't tell you; it's too humiliating. (*He pours another drink*)

Ruth Please.

Gerald (*indicating her drink*) Drink that then.

Ruth Are you about to shock me?

Gerald She makes me feel—well—less than a man.

Ruth Oh, I am sorry, I didn't know.

Gerald What?

Ruth About your peculiarity.

Gerald What peculiarity?

Ruth Well, whatever it is that makes you feel less than a man.

Gerald No, it's not like that. It's just that she won't let me dominate her.

Ruth You mean bully her.

Gerald No, I mean in bed. She has to make all the running. If I become manly, aggressive, she—well, she—giggles.

Ruth (*smiling*) How terrible for you. Poor old "G".

Gerald I'm not poor and I'm not old. I told you ...

Ruth (*holding up her glass*) I think I need another drink.

Gerald (*rising, taking the bottle from the table and sitting beside her*) I should never have told you. I knew all this soul searching would ruin the weekend. Now you'll think I'm inadequate in some way: have something missing that makes women giggle in bed.

Ruth No, of course I won't.

They sit looking at each other, sipping their wine

Gerald There you see: you do, don't you?

Ruth No, don't be silly.

Gerald What are you thinking then?

Ruth (*rising, placing her glass on the table and opening the stairs door*) That you don't understand women. Come on, let's go to bed before the dawn chorus starts.

Gerald (*lost in gloom*) You'll despise me now.

If the inset bedroom is not used, the following lines will be said at the foot of the stairs

---

Ruth (*going up the stairs to the inset bedroom*) Don't talk nonsense. I'll try to explain to you in the morning. (*Calling down*) Are you taking that bottle to bed with you?

Gerald (*coming to*) What? Oh—(*Jumping up and moving to the table*) Right, I'll douse the light then. (*In his haste, he turns the light down but not off and dashes up the stairs. Arriving in inset bedroom*) Oh, Ruth, I need you desperately.
Ruth I thought you might.
Gerald (*embracing her and manœuvring her on to the bed*) You can't let me down after all I've confided.
Ruth (*extricating herself and pulling him to his feet*) Anyway, let's start respectably in two beds, shall we?
Gerald I can't sleep alone tonight. I need the warmth and comfort of a woman.
Ruth Any woman?
Gerald None but you, Ruth. You know that.
Ruth (*pushing him out*) I'll change in here. You go and warm the big bed.
Gerald (*re-appearing*) For us?
Ruth (*pushing him out again*) We'll see.

Gerald goes. There is a short pause in which Ruth fusses with her hair, etc., then a hullabaloo as if from the other bedroom: crashes and bangs, screams from Teresa, shouts from Dora and Gerald. Gerald bursts from the stairs door, hotly pursued by Dora and Teresa in their nighties. Gerald retreats before them to fall on his back. Ruth reacts to the noise but does not leave the bedroom until Gerald has appeared on the stage

Dora (*straddling him*) You dirty peeping Tom you. I'll larn yer! (*To Teresa*) Come on, gal, turn that light up, I want ter see what the dirty old bugger looks like!

Teresa turns up the light and then comes down to Gerald

Teresa What if he's a sex maniac, Mum?
Gerald Get off! Let me explain! You don't ...
Dora Grab his legs, gal!

Teresa darts down and lifts his legs

Gerald Listen, it's all some ghastly mistake!
Dora Made a mistake all right, trying it on with me. We know how ter deal with the likes of you.

Ruth emerges from the stair door and moves to the fireplace, doing her best not to laugh

Teresa (*seeing Ruth and dropping Gerald's legs*) Ooh-er!
Dora (*turning and seeing Ruth*) Who the Hell?
Ruth I think there's been some mistake.
Dora I should bloody well say there has!
Gerald Get off, woman and let me ...
Ruth Are you Mrs Day?
Dora (*letting go of Gerald*) I are. And who might you be?
Teresa What you doing in our house?
Gerald (*levering himself to a sitting position*) I've been assaulted.

Dora (*pushing him down with her foot*) Serves you right!
Teresa (*turning him over with her foot*) What you expect!
Ruth Mr Flack let us the cottage. He said you'd moved to the village.
Dora The old sod, and he made us pay ter the end of the month.
Teresa Bloody old skinflint!
Dora (*turning on her*) I told yer not ter swear, gal!
Ruth (*indicating the sofa*) Come and sit down, Mrs Day. It must have been quite a shock.

Dora sits on the sofa

Gerald (*crawling to the table*) What about me, then? I suppose it's nothing to be set upon by two Amazons. (*He lifts the wine box and sits on the chair by the table*)
Ruth That's better. (*Indicating the sofa*) Your daughter had better sit here.
Dora Teresa.
Ruth Come along, Teresa. I expect you feel a bit shaky, too?
Teresa (*sitting on the sofa*) Not half, I'm all of a dooda. (*To Dora*) What's an Amazon, Mum?
Dora Shut up, gal, don't make things no worse.
Teresa (*looking at Gerald and then back to her mother*) He means you're butch!
Ruth We'll all laugh about this in the morning.
Gerald (*standing, still clutching the box of wine*) I need a drink!
Ruth (*going to the table*) Good idea, let's all have one. (*She pours two drinks*)
Gerald Hurrah, somebody's noticed me. (*Moving above the sofa and speaking to Dora and Teresa*) Well, it may surprise you to know that I only brought two glasses. Silly of me not to have thought of the late-night guests, commonly found lurking in bedrooms in out-of-the-way cottages.
Dora Plenty of glasses in the kitchen, mate.

With a poisonous look at Dora, Gerald stomps up to the kitchen, dumps the wine box and searches for glasses

Ruth Well, it's obvious Mr Flack thought he'd cash in on the empty cottage.
Dora Ain't no right.
Teresa Trust him, crafty old sod.
Dora Watch it, gal!
Ruth It's a bit late for introductions, but I'm Ruth Hill—(*she nods towards the kitchen*)—Mr Turner's secretary. We're down here to do a bit of work on the earthwork.

Gerald returns with two half-pint glasses and pours two large drinks

Dora (*not understanding*) Work on the earthwork, ooh-ar.
Teresa Ploughing?
Ruth No, not exactly, just measuring, perhaps a little digging if we're allowed. You know the big mound up by the spinney, Blue Bell Wood.
Dora "Devil's Hump."
Teresa "Devil's Bum."

Dora Teresa!

Teresa Well, that's what the kids call it. Ain't no good digging there: you won't grow nothing.

Gerald Who wants to grow what?

Dora I know why you're here right enough.

Gerald You do?

Ruth (*picking up two drinks and crossing behind the sofa*) Well, we'll have to make the best of it tonight. (*With a glance at Gerald*) It's too late to do anything now. (*She hands a drink to Dora and Teresa*)

Dora sniffs it

Dora (*handing it back to Ruth*) Not for me, thanks, miss. Can't abide the smell of booze in bed. Reminds me of me old man.

Ruth sits at table and places Dora's glass on it

Teresa I don't mind if I do. (*She drains glass and smacks her lips*) Ooh, not a bad drop of old cider, that.

Gerald winces

Ruth (*picking up one of the glasses of wine she had poured earlier*) Now, I suggest that you, Mrs Day, and your daughter share the double bedroom. I'll have the single and Mr Turner can sleep down here.

Gerald Thank you, that sounds very cosy.

Ruth It's only for tonight, Gerald.

Teresa What about Dad then, Mum?

Ruth Mr Day?

Dora Forgot all about him, gal.

Gerald We're not expecting him are we?

Dora Tom's playing cricket.

Gerald At this time of night?

Teresa He ain't playing now; he's at the boozer.

Gerald (*moving to the fireplace*) Where's he going to sleep then? I'm not having him down here with me.

Dora Don't you worry none, he'll have forgot we've come back here. He'll either go down to our new place or straight ter the farm in time for milking. Depends on whether they wins or loses.

Teresa Slept with Hamish once he did when they won.

Dora Two old bulls together. (*Getting up*) Anyhow, I'm too wore out ter bother. (*To Teresa*) You coming, gal?

Teresa Don't feel tired no more, Mum.

Dora You gotter come, gal, else—(*indicating Gerald*)—he can't get no sleep. Come on! (*She goes to the stairs door*)

Teresa (*rising, going to the table and picking up the bottle of wine*) Reckon I'll have another drop of old Flacky's cider, I will. (*She takes a swig from the bottle*)

Dora (*taking the bottle away from her, putting it on the table and dragging her upstairs*) No, you won't, my girl. Don't want you getting a taste for booze. One in the family's bad enough.

Dora and Teresa disappear up the stairs, leaving the stairs door open

Gerald (*moving to close the stair door, then above the table to put down his glass*) You're not going to do it, are you?

Ruth What?

Gerald Leave me down here, alone.

Ruth What will the Days think if they find us curled up together on the sofa?

Gerald No more than the old biddy thinks now. Stay for a while anyway. You can always creep up later when they're asleep. Come on, it'll probably be our last chance to be alone this week-end. (*Proffering the bottle*) Have some more.

Ruth No thanks. I think I've had more than enough already.

Gerald Just a nightcap.

Ruth (*holding out her glass*) A small one then.

Gerald (*putting the bottle down and switching Ruth's glass for the one discarded by Dora*) This old cider ain't half bad, are it. (*Going up to the kitchen area*) Think I'll open another.

Ruth (*sipping her drink*) Don't open one for me, I'd rather not drink any.

Gerald (*looking in the wine box*) Come to think of it though, I need something stronger. Should be a bottle of whisky—yes. (*He lifts out the whisky bottle*) Would you rather?

Ruth (*rising, turning down the light a little, and drifting over to sit on the sofa*) No thanks. I'll stick to the wine unless you want me to pass out completely.

Gerald (*coming from kitchen area to the table carrying a glass and the bottle of whisky*) Well, I need it, so would you if you'd been savaged. (*Pouring himself a glass of whisky*) Hell, these country women are built like tanks. I shall be sore for a month.

Ruth You'd better not get any ideas about young Teresa then.

Gerald I told you—and I'll tell you something else: that young devil would get sent off in a rugby match, grabbing me where she did. (*Raising his glass*) Well, cheers.

Ruth (*raising her glass*) Cheers.

Gerald switches his glass for hers

Gerald (*coming to the sofa to sit by Ruth*) Here's to peace and quiet.

Ruth (*after a pause*) Gerald, why don't we go home? No harm's been done.

Gerald You weren't grabbed by young Teresa.

Ruth Be serious, to your marriage, I mean. You can always tell Alison it wasn't worth staying.

Gerald You've gone off me, I suppose, since I told you ...

Ruth 'Course not, it's the reverse. (*Draining her glass*) I find you more attractive and with all this damned drink, I'm finding it harder to think of Alison every damned minute.

Gerald (*taking her glass and placing it on the table and then returning above the sofa*) Good. Believe me, if I thought this would harm Alison, I'd go

home at once. (*Leaning over the back of the sofa*) But it won't—she may
even benefit. I'd be so much nicer to live with.

Ruth I want to believe you.

Gerald I'd be less tetchy.

Ruth And you're sure Alison would benefit, are you?

Gerald Unquestionably.

Ruth Right, kiss me!

Gerald (*straightening up*) What?

Ruth Kiss me, take me!

Gerald (*coming round the sofa*) What now?

Ruth Yes, now. Let's go!

Gerald (*closing to her hesitatingly*) But Alison.

Ruth (*drawing him down to her*) To hell with Alison. There's nobody but us
in the whole wide world. Come on, damn you, kiss me!

*A little reluctantly, Gerald enters into a passionate kiss. There is the roar of a
tractor, and headlights flash across the front window*

(*Pushing him away, jumping up and crossing to the window*) Now what!

Gerald (*struggling to his feet*) What the hell's that!

Ruth There are two men. They're coming to the door. (*Moving to the table
and pouring herself another drink*) One of them's old Flack, I can recognize
his walk.

Gerald (*marching to the front door*) Right, I'll just about tell him what I
think. I'm a patient man but this is the last straw! (*He wrenches open the
door*)

Flack and Lionel are standing outside

Why, Mr Flack, how nice to see you.

Ruth goes and lies down full length on the sofa

Flack I was frit yer might have gone and hit the hay.

Ruth Were you? Well it might surprise you to know that that has already
been done by two of your late tenants, the Day women!

Flack (*moving in*) What they back for?

Lionel follows Flack, both taking in Ruth

Gerald (*laughing falsely*) Apparently, the comforts of a modern council house
didn't compare with what they'd been used to, Mr Flack.

Flack Better sort it out like, ain't I? (*Indicating Lionel*) This here's me son.

Gerald Yes do.

Lionel 'Ow do. (*Moving to the sofa, staring at Ruth*) 'Ow do!

Flack (*still staring at Ruth who is draped provocatively on the sofa*) Reckon
as how we come at the wrong time, then.

Lionel (*leering at Ruth*) Or the right time, Dad.

Flack (*turning to Gerald*) Had ter knock yer up 'cause yer parked yer car in
the lane and we can't get the old harvester back ter the farm. Coming at
six they are ter take it ter Bailey's. There'll be hell ter pay if it ain't loaded.

Gerald Right, Mr Flack, I'll go and move it at once. Must keep the wheels turning. (*Calling back as he goes*) Won't be a moment, Ruth.

Gerald exits

Ruth (*still staring at Lionel, fascinated*) No hurry, take your time.

Flack Won't take us long. (*Turning to Lionel*) You can go ahead, boy, and get the gate open.

Lionel continues to leer at Ruth

Hear what I say, Lionel. Wake up, boy, keep yer mind on the job!

Lionel (*still staring at Ruth*) I are, Dad, I are.

Flack exits, thinking Lionel is following

(*Following Flack to the door and closing it after him*) I are. (*Moving back to the end of the sofa*) What's your name, then?

Ruth Ruth.

Lionel (*pointing at his chest*) Lionel.

Ruth How do you do, Lionel.

Lionel Better, gal, for having met you, bit of all right you are. (*Flexing his arm muscle*) 'Ere, feel that.

Ruth What?

Lionel This here, man's muscle that are.

Ruth Very nice.

Lionel Go on, feel it. It won't bite yer.

Ruth (*rising*) Very nice, Lionel.

Lionel Like that all over I are, Ruth.

Ruth (*moving to the table and putting her glass down*) Yes, I'm sure you are, Lionel.

Lionel (*moving to her*) What about it, then?

Ruth What about what?

Lionel (*pulling her violently to him*) This here! (*He kisses her*)

Ruth (*breaking away*) Well, really!

Lionel Never mind, "well really", give us another! (*Pulling her slowly into his arms*) Don't want ter waste time, gal. (*He kisses the struggling Ruth again*)

She stops struggling and enjoys it

The stairs door opens and Dora appears

At the sound of Dora's voice, Lionel releases Ruth

Dora Here, what's all the rumpus, enough ter wake the dead! (*Seeing Lionel*) Lionel, what you at?

Lionel (*backing to the front door*) Bit a chaff in her eye, just got it out fer her. (*Pinching her bottom*) See yer, Ruth.

Lionel exits, closing the door after him

Dora How'd he come ter be here, then?

Ruth (*moving to the fireplace, rubbing her bottom*) Helping his dad to move the harvester. That's what all the noise . . .

Dora (*turning the lamp up to full*) Yer want ter watch that one, gal, oughter have a ring through his nose, he did.

Gerald's car starts up, followed by the roar of the harvester

(*Moving to the front window and peering out*) Never thinks of no-one. Knock yer up any time he would if it suited.

Headlights flash across the window

(*Shouting*) Hope yer run it in the ditch, mean old bugger!

Teresa enters from the stairs, rubbing her eyes

(*Turning back to Ruth*) Beats me how Lil stands him. (*Seeing Teresa*) Woke you an' all, gal, has he?

Teresa What's going on, Mum? Who was you a-shouting at?

Dora Only old Flack, who else would wake yer at this time? (*Moving to the stairs door*) Shan't sleep a wink now, gal. All churned up I are. Might as well get dressed.

Teresa (*sitting at the table*) Coo, old what'sit's opened another bottle of that there cider. (*She picks up the bottle and takes a swig*)

Dora (*sitting at the table*) Pass us a drop, gal, might settle me stomach.

Teresa pours a glass for Dora and then continues to drink from the bottle herself

Ruth (*moving to the table*) Yes, help yourselves. I'm sure Mr Turner won't mind if it will help you sleep. (*Taking the bottle from Teresa*) Excuse me. Let me pour you some. (*She pours two drinks: hands one to Dora and the other to Teresa*) I'd like to offer you a hot drink but we haven't unpacked the gas stove yet.

Dora Cup of Horlicks might help. (*To Teresa*) Put the kettle on, gal.

Lionel opens the back door and peeps in. He then tiptoes up into the kitchen area unseen by the three women

Teresa Range is out, Mum.

Dora Soon boil a kettle with some of that small wood. Go on, gal! (*To Ruth*) Any excuse with them these days.

Teresa goes up to the kitchen area, where she is immediately grabbed by Lionel who kisses her before she can say anything

Ruth (*topping up her glass*) I don't know how you've managed all these years without electricity and mains water.

Dora It's what yer brung up to, ain't it. Be better in the village though, except for the boys chasing our Teresa. All arter her they'll be. Only Lionel out here and I can soon see him off.

Ruth (*moving to the sofa, taking in Teresa and Lionel in a clinch and then dropping down to the fireplace, speaking out front*) You must find Lionel a bit of a handful?

Dora Can't turn me back on 'em, gal, else they'd be at it.

Lionel disengages a hand to wave at Ruth

Ruth I don't think you should blame Teresa, though; Lionel definitely has a sort of animal magic.

Dora Oh, that's what it is, is it? He and our old bull make a good pair.

Gerald enters from the front door

Gerald (*closing the door, so that he does not see Dora*) He could have told me where to park earlier. He must have known he would have to bring that thing up the lane. (*Seeing Dora*) Good God, you're back!

Ruth The noise woke them.

Gerald Them?

Teresa (*breaking away from Lionel and popping her head round the kitchen partition*) Hello, Mr Turner, would you like a cup of Horlicks?

Lionel immediately whips her back out of sight of Gerald

Gerald (*flopping into a chair at the table*) Horlicks, coffee, hemlock, strychnine! Who cares?

Dora (*to Ruth*) Told yer, gal, they're all the same. If things don't go their way, they turn nasty. You're his secretary, ain't yer?

Ruth Well – yes.

Dora Don't need ter stand any of his old buck, then. Tell him ter stick his job. Anyway, what yer here for, working overtime?

There is a little flurry of activity from Lionel and Teresa in the kitchen

Ruth (*directing her attention on Dora with some effort*) We're examining an earthwork.

Dora What fer?

Ruth Mr Turner's trying to prove something to himself. He has a theory.

Dora Thought there was summat up with him.

Gerald (*heaving himself out of the chair and moving above the table*) There's absolutely nothing wrong with me, Mrs Day, that a good night's sleep won't cure. Now do you think we could all go to bed?

Dora (*calling to Teresa*) How's the fire, gal?

Teresa (*breaking out of a clinch with Lionel*) Getting it lit up, Mum.

Dora You ain't forgot ter warm the milk, gal?

Teresa Ain't no milk, Mum.

Gerald (*going rapidly up to the kitchen*) There's milk under the sink. I'll come or it will take all night.

Lionel breaks away from Teresa towards the back door but is not quick enough to avoid being seen by Gerald

Hello, Lionel!

Dora (*staring*) Lionel!

Teresa scoots across to the far side of the table

(*Struggling to get up*) What the 'ell you doing 'ere. Where's my broom!

Lionel (*retreating to the back door*) Dad sent me 'cause we knocked yer up—ter say sorry like.

Dora (*still struggling to rise*) You'll be sorry when I gets at yer, you young ...

Lionel 'Night all. (*Attempting to pinch Ruth's bottom*) See yer, Ruth.

Dora Ruth! Cheeky, young devil. I'll tan his arse afore long, you see if I don't.

Teresa Why'd he call you Ruth?

Dora (*rising and shouting across the table*) 'Cause he don't know no better, gal. Like his old dad he are.

Teresa No he ain't, Mum. You're always on to him you are. Never give him ...

Gerald (*moving to the table, pushing Teresa down into a chair, then hustling Dora down to sit her on the sofa*) If you think I'm staying up half the night listening to you two arguing the pros and cons about Lionel, you've got another think coming! (*Marching up to the kitchen area*) Now, you both sit down while I get the Horlicks.

Dora Here, don't you start pushing us around, this is our house not yourn!

Teresa You can't get it anyhow, fire's gone out.

Gerald (*calling from the kitchen as he pours the milk brought by Debbie*) It's a special recipe, you'll see.

Ruth (*sitting by Dora on the sofa*) He doesn't mean to be rude; he's a little upset, feeling very frustrated.

Teresa He ain't the only one.

Ruth Has a lot on his mind at present.

Dora Only one thing on his mind, as far as I can see. You don't want ter trust him gal, he's got that look in his eye.

Ruth What look?

Dora Can't describe it, gal. Take a look at old Hamish and you'll see what I mean.

Gerald comes down from the kitchen area carrying two mugs, which he places on the table and pours a generous measure of whisky into each

Lionel's got it an' all.

Gerald What has Lionel got?

Teresa (*with a dreamy look on her face*) A lovely body.

Ruth (*with a dreamy look on her face*) Yes, lovely.

Dora Has he? Well, he better keep it to hisself, that's all I can say.

Gerald (*pushing one of the mugs into Teresa's hand*) Two special Horlicks coming up.

Teresa I like it hot.

Gerald (*moving to the fireplace, thrusting the other mug into Dora's hand as he passes*) I bet you do, Teresa, but we can't have everything we want, can we? (*As he gives the mug to Dora*) There, try that. Irish Horlicks, you can't beat it!

Dora (*sipping hers and spluttering*) Thought as much—laced. That won't get yer nowhere with me, mate.

Teresa (*drinking*) Oo-er, nice, ain't it.

Dora (*rising and marching to the stairs door, placing her drink on the table as she goes*) I'm not drinking that there. Going up I are, had enough for one day I has. (*To Teresa*) You coming, gal?

Teresa I ain't finished me drink yet, Mum.

Dora Suit yerself. Don't wake me though, if I've gone off.

Dora goes up the stairs, closing the stairs door behind her

Gerald (*to Teresa*) Come on, now, don't keep your mother waiting.

Teresa Wan't ter get rid of me do yer?

Gerald No, of course not, but . . .

Ruth (*sitting bolt upright*) Gerald, I'm sorry, but I'm afraid I shall have to make a trip down the garden.

Teresa (*topping up her mug with whisky*) What yer want ter do that fer? Pitch-black out there it are.

Ruth I need to excuse myself, that's all.

Teresa What fer? Ain't done nothing wrong as far as I can see.

Gerald Miss Hill means she wants to use the toilet.

Teresa Oh, go ter the boghouse. Could have said then, couldn't she.

Ruth (*to Gerald*) You'll have to come with me, Gerald.

Gerald (*going up to the kitchen*) Right, I'll get a torch. I saw one on the kitchen shelf.

Teresa Ain't room fer two of yer in there.

Ruth (*rising*) I don't mean in with me, Teresa.

Gerald (*coming back from the kitchen with the torch*) Do you want me to come with you?

Ruth No, I don't! Just take a look outside that's all.

Gerald exits through the back door

Teresa Dunno what yer fussing about.

Ruth I don't want that brute breathing down my neck.

Teresa Thought yer said he wasn't going in with yer.

Ruth The bull, your Hamish!

Teresa (*emptying her mug with a long drink*) Oo-ar, what's the difference?

Gerald returns

Gerald All's quiet. Away you go.

Ruth (*taking the torch from him*) Right, won't be a minute. Leave the door open.

Ruth exits

Gerald goes to Teresa, who sits staring into space in a drunken stupor. He takes the mug from her hand which remains suspended in mid-air. He passes his hand in front of her eyes without any reaction. Then, he tries lifting her limp left hand. As he does so, the suspended right one flops to the table. He lets go of her left hand and the right pops up again as the left drops limply to her side

Gerald (*pulling Teresa to her feet*) Come along, Teresa, time for beddy byes. (*He gets behind her and steers her up to the stair door*) That's it, keep going!

Teresa (*breaking from him and reeling towards the table*) Get orf! Haven't finished me drink, have I? (*She staggers*) Ooh-er, don't half feel giddy, I do. (*She spins round and totters to the armchair*) Better sit down, I had. (*She flops into the armchair*)

Gerald (*rushing down and pulling her to her feet*) No, no, Teresa, you must go to bed! to *bed*, do you hear? (*He gets behind her and pushes her towards the stair door*)

Teresa (*with slurred speech*) Uncle "G" wants to take Teresa to bed, does he?

Gerald Yes ... (*breaking away below the sofa*) No! (*Turning to her*) Who told you about Uncle "G"?

Teresa (*advancing on him*) Debbie says you're a great big, cuddly Uncle "G".

Gerald (*backing away from her*) Does she? I was like an uncle, like an uncle, you understand, Teresa!

Teresa (*beckoning him*) Naughty Uncle "G", give Teresa a kiss.

Gerald (*moving to her*) Please, Teresa, you must go to bed with your mother!

Teresa (*Pushing him down on to the sofa*) I'd rather go on the sofa with you. (*Leaping on top of him*) Love me, Uncle "G"!

Gerald (*struggling free and rising*) Good Lord, are there no morals left? This is promiscuity taken to the point of indecency! (*Taking her hand and pulling her to her feet*) You're a lovely girl, Teresa, but you see I'm a married man and ...

Teresa She won't know nothing.

Gerald (*backing away from her*) They always know, Teresa, they always know.

Teresa You ain't too old, are yer?

Gerald (*continuing to back away*) Yes, I am, Teresa, much too old for you.

Teresa (*advancing on him*) Mum says dirty old men ain't never too old.

Gerald (*adopting a Victorian father pose*) Now, look here, my girl. This has gone far enough!

Teresa (*putting her arms round his neck*) No it ain't, Uncle "G", not yet it ain't.

Ruth enters through the back door and stares at them

Ooh, I don't half feel randy (*passing out and hanging limply from his neck*).

Gerald becomes aware of Ruth

Ruth Doing our good night daddy bit, are we?

Gerald No, I'm not. She's as tight as a tick. Give me a hand, will you!

Ruth (*crossing to help him*) You've only yourself to blame, putting all that whisky in her drink.

Teresa (*coming to and throwing an arm round each of their necks*) Your wife's nice. She won't mind—(*to Ruth*)—won't mind, will you, if I borrows your Hamish?

Ruth (*grinning at Gerald*) Please help yourself.

Gerald For God's sake, let's get her upstairs.

They half carry her up the stairs. If the inset bedroom is not used, the following dialogue will be said off

Ruth I'm trying to but she's so limp.
Gerald I'll go first, you bring up the rear. Just steady her, will you? Keep her moving for God's sake!

They appear in the inset bedroom

Teresa My Mum'll get her old broom ter you, she will.
Gerald She'll have to go in the small bed.
Teresa I don't half go in any old bed.

They struggle to get her on the bed

> *The back door bursts open and Lionel appears, supporting a very drunk Mr Day. He is still wearing a single batting pad and obviously imagines he is still on the cricket field. He attempts to swing his arm, muttering " 'Ow's zat!"*

Lionel struggles to force him up the stairs but he resists, breaks free and staggers downstage, where he mimes bowling a ball across the room. He then lurches across and pretends to play the ball. Finally, he takes up the fielder's role, watching the ball dropping to him from a great height. With a triumphant " 'Ow's zat!" he collapses on the sofa. Lionel nips up into the kitchen area as he hears Gerald and Ruth descending the stairs

Gerald (*emerging from the stairs and moving above the table*) The old girl was dead to the wide, thank heaven.
Ruth (*following him and sitting at table*) So's your girlfriend.

Lionel darts out from the kitchen area and nips up the stairs, unseen by Gerald and Ruth, closing the door after him

Gerald (*sitting on the chair above the table*) I'm sorry, Ruth, darling, it's all been a bit of a fiasco, hasn't it?
Ruth You could say that.
Gerald Am I forgiven?
Ruth I suppose so.
Gerald Let's have a little nightcap.
Ruth Very little then, I'm not going down the garden again for anyone.
Gerald (*picking up Dora's abandoned mug*) Perhaps you'd like to try my special Horlicks.
Ruth No thanks. I've seen what that can do.

Gerald pours two drinks from the opened wine bottle and they sit sipping them. Lionel appears in the inset bedroom. He has already taken off his shirt. He quickly slips off his trousers and climbs into bed with Teresa. She wakes, strikes out wildly saying "Dirty old man", scrambles out of bed and disappears out of the bedroom. Lionel pulls the sheets over his head and settles down to sleep

> *Teresa exits*

Script to be used if the inset bedroom is not included
Teresa (*off*) Get off, you dirty old man!
Lionel (*whispering*) It's me, Teresa, Lionel.
Teresa (*off, loudly*) No it ain't, I know who you are! I'm going in with my mum.
Lionel (*off, loudly*) Come back, gal, it are me, honest. Oh, damn yer then!

Ruth I think Teresa's having a nightmare. I think you're in it.
Gerald Please shut up about Teresa, Ruth. I've had enough of her for one night.
Ruth But not enough of me, is that it?
Gerald Ruth, you know how I feel about you. Please don't tease me any more.
Ruth What about Alison?
Gerald We've settled all that. Now are you going to let me make love to you or not?
Ruth I think I would quite like to but ...
Gerald (*placing his finger on her lips*) No more "buts". Look, I'm going to pop down to the little wooden hut. Go and drape yourself on the sofa (*Moving to the back door*) and prepare to meet your fate, mate.

Gerald exits, laughing and beating his chest

Ruth (*rising and shouting after him*) Watch out for your pal, Hamish, or you'll meet your fate mate. (*She freezes on the last word as she suddenly sees the inert Mr Day curled up on the sofa, recovers and starts to run after Gerald*) Gerald! Gerald!

Before she gets to the back door, she stops and walks thoughtfully back to above the sofa where she stands looking down on the drunken Mr Day. Slowly she starts to grin as an idea strikes her. Grinning to herself, she collects her handbag from the armchair and goes to the table, where she sits and writes a short note. She then goes to the fireplace, props the note on the mantelpiece and with a last look towards the back door, she goes up the stairs, collecting her handbag as she passes the table. As she closes the door, the drunken Tom groans and lurches over so that his hand grips the top of the sofa, making the tips of his fingers visible to Gerald on his return. Ruth appears in the inset bedroom and crosses to sit on the bed to remove her shoes. Lionel sits up behind her and clamps his arms round her waist. She freezes as she looks down at his hands.

Teresa?
Lionel (*as he pulls her into the bed*) O.K. kid, quit struggling and take what's coming to yer!

They disappear under the bedclothes

Script to be used if the inset bedroom is not included
Ruth (*off*) Teresa? Lionel! What are you ...?
Lionel (*off*) O.K. kid, quit struggling and take what's coming to yer!
Ruth (*off*) Stop it, Lionel! Do you hear! Lionel, you—Lionel, you—Oh, Lionel.

Gerald enters, closes the back door and turns the key

Gerald Everything's quiet outside. (*Walking across to the table, lightly brushing Tom's fingers as he does so*) That's it, my sweet, relax. Big "G" will put out the light and then it'll be sheer heaven. (*He turns out the lamp*)

The whole stage is left in darkness

(*feeling his way to the sofa*) I shall always remember tonight, my love. I shall count it as one of the great experiences of my life. Now ... Ouch! Ouch!
Mr Day 'Ow's zat!

CURTAIN

ACT II

SCENE 1

The same. 11 a.m. the next morning

When the Curtain rises the stage is empty. On the table is the remains of breakfast: the end of a loaf of bread, butter on a plate, a marmalade jar, a large tea pot, a sugar bowl, four used plates and cups and one of each still unused. The kitchen door is open and Dora appears with a shopping bag. She puts it down in the kitchen and walks down above the table

Dora (*with hands on hips, surveying the uncleared table*) Well, I'd go to ... (*She marches up to the stairs door and shouts*) Teresa, you staying in bed all bloomin' day? You don't come now, gal, I'll come up there and tan yer arse, growed as yer are!

Teresa (*off*) Keep yer hair on, Mum, can't go no quicker, can I?

Dora You want me up there with my broom?

Teresa (*off*) All right, all right, hang on, don't get yerself in a flummix.

Dora I'll flummix yer, gal, yer don't get a move on!

Teresa (*off*) Said I was coming, din't I? Ain't got more than one pair of hands, have I?

Dora (*moving to the kitchen to put down the shopping bag*) Cheek me, gal, and I'll give yer a thump round the ear'ole to be going on with!

Teresa emerges from the stair door looking very much the worse for wear

Teresa (*holding her head and moving above the table*) Ooh, ain't half got a terrible head, Mum.

Dora (*from the kitchen*) What comes of spending half the day in bed.

Teresa (*sitting at the table*) No it ain't, it's that old cider what done it.

Dora (*coming down to the table*) You want summat ter eat, yer better get it now, 'cause I ain't waiting no longer afore I clears this pigsty.

Teresa Bit of bread and marmalade'll do and a cup of tea.

Dora (*piling up the dirty plates*) Fine time of day this are ter be eating yer breakfast. Ain't got a lot of time for young Lionel but I'll say one thing for him, he ain't idle. Up afore me he were. (*Taking the dirty dishes up to the kitchen*) Found him down here trying ter wake yer dad fer milking.

Teresa He come home then?

Dora Lionel?

Teresa No, Dad.

Dora Not as yer'd notice; slumped on that sofa he were at six this morning with a smile on his face like an old Cheshire cat.

Teresa What about him then?

Dora Who, yer dad?

Teresa No, old Turner; where'd he sleep then?

Dora (*returning to the table, pouring a cup of tea, cutting bread, etc.*) In that there old chair, snoring fit ter wake the dead. Din't think a lot on it either, ter judge by his old temper when he woke up—in a right old state he were. She were all right though, said she'd had a good night, very good, she said.

Teresa They gone out then have they, them two?

Dora 'Bout nine. Went up ter "Devil's Hump". Don't ask me what fer.

Teresa Bet I knows what fer: wants what he couldn't get here.

Dora You get on with yer breakfast; you're a sight too forrard, gal. I don't hold with it. (*She takes some more of the breakfast things out to the kitchen*)

Teresa Mum, was you awake when I come up ter bed?

Dora (*from the kitchen*) No, I wan't, and what time was it when you come up?

Teresa Dunno, don't remember going ter bed. Well, not much—her and him was helping me up the stairs, remember that. Don't remember getting undressed though—Mum? Here, you don't think . . .?

Dora (*coming down to collect some more breakfast things*) Shouldn't wonder.

Teresa What him as well as her?

Dora Could have done.

Teresa She wouldn't let him, would she?

Dora Old enough ter be yer father.

Teresa Ooh-er, shan't dare look at him. He said that.

Dora What?

Teresa 'Bout being old enough ter be me father.

Dora Did he then and what was you a doing?

Teresa I dunno, do wish I could remember what happened last night. Reckon she let him see me starkers? She wouldn't, would she?

Dora I dunno what she'd do, do I? All I know is, you made a right spectacle on yerself. (*Moving towards the kitchen*) Shouldn't worry none though, I 'spect he's seen more than that. (*Turning back to her*) If he ain't he's a poor old sod and no mistake. You going ter be messing at that table all day? I done a morning's work afore you was up. (*Going to the sink*) Come on, gal, we'd better do something about dinner, case yer dad comes home.

Teresa Wish I could remember.

The front door bursts open and Lily Flack appears, carrying a basket of vegetables

Lily Ooh, ooh, Dora, you about!

Dora (*from the kitchen*) That you, Lily? (*She comes down to Lily*)

Lily Brought yer a few veges, gal. (*Seeing Teresa*) You ain't still having breakfast, Teresa? Proper lady of leisure, ain't we?

Dora I'll give her lady, gal, I can tell yer, if she don't move herself. What's up then? Ain't like you ter bring us veges. (*She takes the basket from Lily and dumps it on the kitchen sink*)

Lily Thought I'd pop along, gal, ter see how you was a managing. Bill told me as how you was back. Well, what happened then?

Dora (*returning to Lily*) What yer mean?

Lily When you walked in on old Turner.

Dora Long story, gal. Teresa, put the kettle on. You'll stay for a cuppa, Lil, won't yer?

Lily (*moving to the front door*) Ain't got time, gal, all behind as it are.

Teresa You should have seen our mum when old Turner crept in her bedroom.

Dora (*cuffing her*) Teresa!

Lily (*stopping and turning*) He done what?

Teresa 'Course he didn't know she was there.

Lily (*sitting at table*) Shouldn't think he did. What a rum old do. Reckon as how I will have that there cuppa arter all, gal.

Dora (*pushing Teresa to her feet and handing her a plate and a cup*) Go and put the kettle on, gal.

Teresa Mum, I want ter tell her.

Dora She'll hear quite enough from me. Go on now, stove's hot, all yer got ter do is fill the kettle.

Teresa goes up reluctantly to the kitchen

Lily What was he at then, gal?

Dora (*sitting at the table*) She was with him—don't take a lot of imagination do it?

Lily Thought it was like that; said ter Bill, they're here for a dirty week-end. I know what he is: sight too friendly with young Debbie he were when he was staying down the farm last year.

Dora Ooh-er, you don't think, gal . . .? (*Counting on her fingers*) How long is it since he was here, September, October, November . . .?

Lily Twelve month, worked it out, I did.

Dora (*with obvious disappointment*) Oh, more likely to have been Lionel then, arter all. Sorry, Lil. I didn't mean . . .

Lily You shouldn't listen to them old gossips, Dora Day. Come ter that, I've heard a few things 'bout her. (*She nods toward the kitchen to indicate Teresa*)

Teresa (*from the kitchen*) What's that about Lionel, Mum?

Dora (*shouting back*) Little pitchers have long ears. You mind yer business, gal, and get that there tea.

There is a knock on the door

Now who the hell's that? Can't be them back; they wouldn't knock anyhow, reckon as how they own the place. (*Struggling to her feet*) Sit down, Lil, I'll see who it are. (*She opens the front door*)

Alison Turner, dressed in the uniform of a district nurse, stands outside

Yes, did yer want summat?

Alison Oh, I seem to have come to the wrong cottage. I'm looking for a Mr Turner.

Dora He ain't here.

Alison I see - perhaps I took a wrong turning. This isn't Mr Flack's cottage?

Dora He ain't here, neither.

Alison You know Mr Flack?

Dora I knows him all right.

Alison Well, perhaps ...

— **Lily** Tell her ter come in, Dora.

Dora Better come in then.

Alison enters, looking around. Dora closes the door

Like a cup of tea, would yer?

Alison That would be nice, thank you.

Dora Sit on the old sofa then and I'll get yer one. (*Shouting*) Teresa, that tea ready yet?

Teresa (*from the kitchen*) Won't be long, Mum.

Dora We'll need an extra cup, gal!

Teresa pours out four cups of tea in the kitchen

Alison You have company, perhaps I should ...

Dora (*waving her hand at Lily*) Only Lil—oh, yes, this here's Lily Flack. What did yer say yer name was?

Alison I didn't, but it's Alison Turner. How do you do, Mrs Flack. You're not the wife of the Mr Flack I was looking for?

— **Lily** Yes I are. Pleased ter meet yer, I'm sure.

Dora (*sitting at the table*) Tell her who I are then, gal.

— **Lily** Ooh-ar. (*Waving her hands towards Dora*) This her's Dora Day; she lives here.

Alison (*sitting on the sofa*) Oh, well, there seems to be some mix up. I'm looking for a cottage that my husband rented for the week-end but, obviously, if Mrs Day lives here, this can't be it.

Dora ⎫
            ⎬ It are. ⎧ *Speaking*
— **Lily** ⎭   ⎩ *together*

— **Lily** Proper old mess there's been. My old man's fault.

Dora Thought we'd left it, he did, so he let it. Paid the rent we had, too, till the end of the month.

Alison So this is the right cottage. You've seen my husband?

Dora Not 'alf, we have.

Alison Well, do you know where he is now?

Teresa (*loudly, from the kitchen*) "Devil's Bum"!

Alison I beg your pardon?

Dora She means "Devil's Hump", it's an 'ill.

Alison (*suddenly understanding*) Oh, the earthwork.

Dora That's what he called it, yes.

Alison So there really is an earthwork. I wonder, do you know if my husband's coming back for lunch?

Dora Shouldn't think so. Takes half an hour ter get up there. Wouldn't be worth coming back fer elevenses.

Alison Eleven - no, I meant for dinner.

Dora Didn't say. I ain't getting nothing, ain't the housekeeper yer know.

— **Lily** Most likely he'll go ter the *Red Lion*. Likes of him usually do.

Alison I see, well I won't be able to—on duty again at one. A friend relieved me this morning so I could pop down here. He wasn't expecting me.

— **Lily** Din't think he was, somehow.

Alison Just thought I'd surprise him.
Dora You'd have done that right enough.
Alison Of course, Mrs Day being in residence here has rather spoilt the fun.
Lily Not 'alf, it has.
Alison He's helpless on his own, you know. I'm afraid I've rather spoilt him.
Dora Would be helpless on his own.
Alison I suppose I've been silly really but—well, we've never been apart since we married. Took over where his mother left off, I suppose. But I'm sure he's perfectly capable.
Dora Should think he's capable all right. Most of 'em are, gal.
Alison Still, I'm sorry to have missed him but please don't tell him I called. I might still get a chance to surprise him.
Dora } Hope yer do, gal, hope yer do. { *Speaking*
Lily }   { *together*

Teresa arrives with two cups of tea, already poured. She goes to the top of the table and puts them down

Dora (*to Alison*) This here's me daughter, Teresa.
Alison Hello.
Teresa (*as she goes up to the kitchen to fetch the other two cups*) Pleased ter meet yer.
Dora (*rising and handing a cup to Alison*) Take sugar, do yer?
Alison No, thank you.
Dora You'd better drink it while it's still warm. (*Returning to her seat*) Like as not, she didn't let the kettle boil.
Alison (*after a pause while she sips her tea*) You're really off the map here. I sometimes wish I could get away from it all.
Lily All what?
Alison This dreadful rat-race.
Lily You gottem in your house an' all, have yer?
Alison Got what?
Dora } Rats! { *Speaking*
Lily }   { *together*
Alison (*laughing*) No, I meant the hustle and bustle, too many people, all trying to out-do one another.

Teresa brings in the other two cups

Teresa (*plonking one cup in front of Dora and then sitting at the table with her own cup*) Here yer are. Hope yer like it strong.
Dora Ain't we got no biscuits, gal?
Teresa We didn't bring none, mum.
Dora (*to Alison*) We only come back for a night or two, ter let the paint dry off a bit.
Lily They got a new council house, see.
Alison (*to Lily*) So that's why your husband let the cottage to Mr Turner?
Dora Yes, crafty old sod.
Teresa Mum!
Dora Well, he are.

Teresa You're allus telling me not ter swear, Mum.

Debbie knocks and enters

Hello, Debbie.

Lily You don't want ter take no notice of her, Mrs Turner—poor old Dora's been under a bit of a strain. (*To Debbie*) What yer want, gal?

Debbie That old bull's trapped that there inspector man: jumped in with the pigs he has; shouting for help he is. Shall I let him be or what?

Lily Leave him be, gal. Nosey old bugger, he are.

Dora Language, Lil!

Alison A little strong language is good sometimes - you should hear some of my pregnant mums when they're having a rough time.

Teresa That your job then, bornin' babies?

Alison Part of it, Teresa, I'm a district nurse.

Teresa (*looking at Debbie*) Plenty of work for yer round here.

Debbie giggles

Lily All right, gal, I'll sort it out when I comes.

Debbie exits

Teresa Hard graft, nursing, wouldn't do fer me. I want ter be a secretary like that there Miss Hill.

Alison You wouldn't like being cooped up in an office all day, Teresa, surely?

Teresa Well, Ruth ain't in no office, are she.

Dora You ain't no business ter call her Ruth, my gal. She's Miss Hill ter you.

Alison Ruth Hill. I have an old friend of that name. She's a librarian now at the university where my husband works.

Lily (*quickly*) Plenty of Hills round here, ain't there, Dora? People I mean.

Dora Can think of six straight off.

Alison Yes, of course, it's a common name. Well—(*rising and handing her cup to Dora*)—I'd better get away. It's nearly a two-hour drive. Thank you, that was very nice.

Dora Sorry you missed him. (*To Lily*) Ain't we, gal.

Lily Ooh-ar.

Dora rises and goes to open the front door

Alison (*tidying her hair in the mirror over the fireplace*) Never mind, I could get relieved at six so if I'm not too tired, I might pop down late tonight. (*Turning to Dora*) Sleeping would be difficult though, I suppose?

Dora Difficult here, any time.

Lily Could let you have a room at the farm if yer want one.

Alison Well, I'll think about it. Would be nice to surprise him though.

Teresa Wouldn't half give him a shock.

Dora cuffs her

Alison (*crossing to the door*) Yes, well thank you for the tea again. (*Turning at the door, speaking to Lily*) I might take you up on that offer of a bed, if the traffic's not too bad. I'm sure my husband's already missing his creature comforts.

Teresa laughs. Dora tries to cuff her again but she dodges and runs up to the kitchen area, laughing

Bye then, may see you later.

Alison exits

Dora (*closing the door and returning above the table to sit*) Hope she catches him at it. Serve him right.

Lily (*sitting at the table*) Better she don't know, gal. If I knew what my old man gets up to, I'd likely shoot him. Still, I'm safe enough, I reckon, seeing as they don't pay men for it.

Teresa (*calling from the kitchen*) Should have told her, Mum.

Dora Ain't none of our business, gal. You get those veges sorted, case yer dad comes home early.

Lily That reminds me, gal, I was supposed ter tell yer he will be home early. He's talked Bill inter giving him the afternoon off so as he can play in the away match at Flitton.

Dora Playing again, are he? Last time they went ter Flitton it was rained off. Took him till two in the morning ter get home though.

Lily Said he might stay with his cousin, Bert, and come home tomorrow morning.

Dora And I knows what that means right enough.

Flack enters from the back door

Lily Feel sorry for you, gal. Suppose I'm lucky my old devil's too mean ter drink much.

Flack (*crossing to Lily*) There yer are, ruddy nattering as usual. Hamish's out again and I can't catch the old bugger no how. Well, don't just sit there, woman, come and give us a hand!

Dora (*rising and moving towards the back door*) I'll come an' all, Bill, seeing as how I kept Lily talking. (*At the door, to Teresa*) Teresa, you get them veges done, case yer dad comes in afore I'm back.

Dora exits

Flack (*calling after her*) Thanks, Dora (*To Lily, who has not moved*) Come on, woman, shift yerself – he'll be half-way to Bexton by now!

Lily (*rising and ambling towards the back door*) Ain't woman's work, catching bulls ain't.

Flack (*as he follows her out*) Lionel ain't around, never is when yer want him. That's you spoiling him, that is.

Lily If you wan't too mean ter put up a decent fence.

Lily and Flack go out

Flack (*off*) Hurry up, will yer, or he'll get hisself killed.

Lily (*off*) It's only your jawing that's stopping us.

> *As soon as their voices have died away, the front door opens and Lionel peers in. Seeing the coast is clear, he creeps into the room*

Lionel (*calling*) Teresa, Teresa, it's me, Lionel.

Teresa (*coming out of the kitchen area to him*) What yer want? Yer dad's been looking for you.

Lionel I know. Thought as how I'd keep out of sight. Saw yer mum go off, so here I are.

Teresa Well, yer can just sling yer hook, Lionel Flack. I know what you are.

Lionel What yer gettin' at?

Teresa Go on back ter yer fancy bit. That's what you can do.

Lionel (*referring to Ruth*) She didn't tell on me, did she?

Teresa (*thinking of Debbie*) Didn't need to, did she? Don't make out you ain't noticed! Like a barn she are.

Lionel Like a barn? Who Ruth?

Teresa Ruth? No, Debbie! You ain't been messing with her too, have yer?

Lionel Who, Debbie.

Teresa No, Ruth!

Lionel (*moving below the sofa*) Dunno what yer mean.

Teresa Oh, Lionel Flack! You ought ter be dealt with, you did, like one of yer dad's bullocks!

Lionel You got it all wrong, you have. Been listening to a lot of old gossip.

Teresa I ain't as daft as yer think. I heard what yer said.

Lionel I never said nothing about Debbie. You brought her into it.

Teresa You've let it out proper now, you have. Old enough ter be yer mother, she are.

Lionel Debbie's same age as me.

Teresa I ain't talkin' about her, are I? Talkin' about you and that Ruth bit!

Lionel What Ruth bit?

Teresa (*attacking him and pushing him on to the sofa*) I hate you, Lionel Flack! Hate you, I do. You can keep your experiences for someone else; I don't want them!

> *Gerald enters from the back door*

Gerald Hello, anybody about? I just popped back to pick up the car. (*He stops as he catches sight of Lionel and Teresa fighting on the sofa*) Oh, sorry…

> *Teresa wrenches herself free, races to the front door and turns to face Gerald*

Teresa And you're another one, both as bad as one another, you are! I'm going after Hamish, I are, be a lot safer with him!

> *Teresa exits, closing the door after her*

Gerald (*looking down on Lionel*) Having a little trouble with our technique, are we?

Lionel (*sitting up*) Trouble? 'Course I ain't, just working her up for later, that's all. Allus works: get 'em angry with yer and yer half-way there.

Gerald (*amused*) Really? Can't say I've ever heard of that.

Lionel No, well, you ain't had the experience, 'ave yer? How did yer get on up there, then?

Gerald Up there?

Lionel "Devil's 'ump".

Gerald The gorse bushes made it very difficult.

Lionel Oh-ar, they would.

Gerald Hard to follow the contours.

Lionel Gorse bushes never stopped me.

Gerald You interested in archaeology? I would never have guessed.

Lionel Arky what? Did you manage to get a little bit of the other up there, then?

Gerald Are you implying that I took Miss Hill up to "Devil's Hump" to seduce her?

Lionel Well, din't yer?

Gerald No, of course I didn't – well, not exactly.

Lionel What fer then?

Gerald Miss Hill takes notes.

Lionel (*really sitting up*) Ooh-ar, real kinky that are. What else she do?

Gerald Look, I don't mind admitting to you, Lionel, as one man to another, that my intentions were not, strictly speaking, honourable. I was hoping for ...

Lionel A bit of the other.

Gerald I was going to say a warm response.

Lionel She's warm all right. I'd call her bloomin' hot stuff.

Gerald (*making a move towards him*) Now, look here, I'm not having you use coarse expressions like that about Miss Hill. She's not one of your little village floozies who'd hop into bed at the drop of a hat.

Lionel All right, keep yer hair on, mate. I know she ain't. I ain't got no hat. Women are all the same though, if yer know how ter handle them.

Gerald I suppose you do with your years of experience.

Lionel Either yer got it or yer ain't. I has – got it.

Gerald (*sarcastically*) Do tell me about your approach, Lionel. I suppose you only have to beckon and they're in bed with you before you can say "Jack Robinson."

Lionel (*missing the sarcasm*) Wouldn't need no help from him neither.

Gerald Well, well, give me a few details, Lionel. This is an opportunity not to be missed. Hang on–(*taking out some paper from his pocket together with a pencil*)–I'll make a few notes, if you don't mind. Don't want to miss anything. Right, fire away.

Lionel What yer want ter know?

Gerald All of it. How to tackle women. (*Pulling him to his feet*) Come on, you can't lecture sitting down. (*He pushes Lionel away and sits on the sofa with his pencil poised in mock expectancy*)

Lionel (*standing awkwardly*) Well, women don't want the old chat, neither, see. You gotter get them going: pitch in strong, don't take no for an answer. (*He flexes his muscles and scowls*) Get 'em ter feel yer muscle.

Gerald (*writing*) "The strong man approach".

Lionel (*demonstrating*) Then yer want ter grab 'em to yer so they can feel yer 'ard body'.

Gerald (*writing*) "Grab 'em close so they can feel yer 'hard body." Yes?

Lionel (*miming*) Then shove 'em off and shout, "Go on, look me straight between the thighs!"

Gerald (*writing*) Shove them off, shout, "Look me straight between the thighs". I like that, very direct.

Lionel (*miming again*) Then pull them back to yer, put yer arm round them so they can't struggle and breathe hard on their necks.

Gerald (*writing*) "Pull towards, clamp with arms—(*in dialect*)—breathe 'ard on neck". What's that supposed to do?

Lionel Erroneous zone that are, gets 'em panting.

Gerald Panting! Good. (*He makes a note*)

Lionel Then yer says, "O.K. kid, quit struggling, there ain't no going back now!" (*He runs to the front door, turns, "paws the ground" with his feet and charges to dive on top of Gerald on the sofa*)

Gerald (*standing up just before Lionel reaches him and continuing to write on the mantelpiece*) "Quit struggling". Should you have soft background music when you say that?

Lionel Eh?

Gerald Never mind. Then what?

Lionel That's it, mate. Either they gives in or they don't.

Gerald I see. How does one know whether they've given in?

Lionel (*rising and miming*) You'll know all right. If they don't, you'll have tears in yer eyes, so yer will.

Gerald (*still enjoying the joke, putting the notes into his inside pocket*) Right. (*Moving to Lionel*) Here we go then—see if I've got it. (*He mimes in an effeminate way*) Grab her close so she can feel my hard muscles. Shove her away. Shout, "Look me straight between the thighs." (*Pulling Lionel to him and using him to practise on*) Breathe 'ard on neck and say, "O.K. kid, quit struggling".

Lionel breaks free

Lionel Here, what are yer, a bloomin' poufter? (*Grabbing Gerald's wrists and pulling him to him*) You gotter make it real strong, not like you was doing it.

Gerald Right, you asked for it! (*He pulls Lionel violently to him*)

Lionel Here!

Gerald (*bending him back*) O.K., kid, there's no going back now. (*He flings him on to the sofa, charges across to the front door, turns, "paws the ground", and takes a running jump on to Lionel*)

As he does so, Tom Day enters from the back door and stands open-mouthed, watching them

Lionel Get orf, you stupid git!

CURTAIN

SCENE 2

The same. 8 p.m. the same day

When the Curtain rises, the stage is empty but immediately the bellow of the bull is heard, and Debbie shrieking off. She bursts through the front door, turns, slams it shut and leans with her back to it, gasping for breath. There is a second bellow much nearer and a banging on the front door

Lionel (*off*) Deb, you ain't locked it have yer! Open it quick or he'll have me! (*Banging on the door again*) Come on, Deb, don't be stupid, open that bloomin' door!

Debbie (*shouting*) Serve you right, Lionel Flack. You said you wan't frit on him so go on then, drive him off!

Lionel (*off*) He's mad at me, Deb. He don't take no notice when he's mad!

Debbie Who's a great Spanish bull-fighter now then?

Lionel (*off*) Deb! He's looking at me again—open that blinkin' door will yer! He's going ter charge, he are!

The bull roars again: this time very close

(*off*) Ooh-ooh-er, help!

Lionel shouts and screams as he charges round the back of the set, to tumble in through the back door which he slams shut behind him

The bull roars as Lionel runs

(*Breathless, leaning against the back door*) Beat yer then, yer silly old sod! (*Moving up and shaking his fist out of the kitchen window*) Ain't frit of you; take more than that ter put the wind up me!

Debbie What yer like then, when yer got the wind up?

Lionel (*ignoring her and peering out of the window*) He's trotted off. Knows when he's beat, I'll say that for him.

Debbie You was frit ter death, you was, same as me.

Lionel (*mopping his brow and coming down to sit on the arm of the sofa*) Don't you tell, gal, that he got me on the run or I shan't never hear the end on it.

Debbie (*moving to him holding her bulge*) I got more than that what I can split on about you, Lionel Flack. When yer going ter tell yer dad about us, then?

Lionel (*falling back on the sofa*) We agreed, Deb, arter it's born. You know me mum goes soft on babies.

Debbie And she'll get round yer dad?

Lionel Yeah, it's better than a big row.

Debbie You won't let me down, will yer, Lionel?

Lionel What me? 'Course I won't, Deb. Soon as anything starts, I'll take yer up to the hospital in Dad's Land Rover. So don't you fret about it.

Debbie (*holding her bulge*) Better make sure it's got some petrol in it then, that's all I can say. Ooh, heck, I think summat's happening: keep getting these funny pains.

Lionel (*jumping up, going to her and throwing her on to the sofa*) Sit quiet a moment and it'll go off.

Debbie Lot you know about it.

Lionel What you expect, I'm a man, ain't I?

Debbie (*holding her bulge*) Have to admit that, seeing as you caused this.

Lionel (*moving to the front door*) You wait here. I'll go and get the Land Rover and whip yer up to the hospital.

Debbie (*holding her bulge*) Ooh-er, I'll never make it, I won't. Reckon you better get some help, Lionel.

Lionel (*falling back to rest against the table, mopping his brow*) Oh, lor, why'd this have ter happen ter me?

Debbie It ain't happening to you as far as I can see. Your fault anyhow, if you hadn't got old Hamish all steamed up, I wouldn't have ter have run, would I?

Lionel (*with new hope*) False alarm, that's what it are. Heard me mum say it often happens.

Debbie (*groaning*) Lionel, you'll have ter get someone. It's happening!

Lionel (*moving to her*) 'Ang about, Debbie, you can't have it here.

Debbie Take more than you to stop it.

Lionel (*helping her up and pushing her towards the stairs*) You go and lie quiet on the bed and perhaps it'll go off.

Debbie (*as they go up the stairs*) You'll get help, though?

All Lionel's following speech will be said "off" if the inset bedroom is not used

Lionel (*as they mount the stairs*) 'Course I will. I'll tell Auntie Dora and she'll look after yer while I fetches a doctor. (*Appearing in the inset bedroom*) Go on, then, get on the bed! (*He helps her roughly into bed*) Steady, gal, take it easy. Don't make things no worse than what they is. (*Leaving her, then popping his head back through the doorway*) Just hold yer breath for five minutes, perhaps it'll go off. (*He thunders down the stairs, closes the stair door and leans with his back against it*)

Ruth enters through the back door

Ruth Hello, Lionel, you here again? And who's the lucky girl today?

Lionel What?

Ruth Upstairs, who have you up there this time?

Lionel Me? Ain't got no-one. Why should I have?

Ruth Teresa's not up there then?

Lionel No, she ain't; she's gone arter Hamish.

Ruth (*moving below the table and resting against it*) Deserted you for Hamish, has she? Sensible girl.

Lionel attempts to sidle out of the back door

Lionel! No need to run away, Mr Turner won't be in for a minute: he's fiddling with the car.

Lionel Look, I gotta go, important work like. (*He backs towards the door*)

Ruth Just a minute, I want to say something to you.

Lionel (*moving back reluctantly, miming and pointing to the bedroom*) I can't meet yer tonight, if that's …

Ruth No, it's not that: I want you to know, Lionel, that last night was a once and for all experience; definitely not to be repeated, so don't go talking about it to anyone, understand? No boasting to your friends!

Lionel (*closing with her*) Me, boast? Good though, wan't I?

Ruth You were one of life's experiences, Lionel, that's all.

Lionel Ooh-ar!

Ruth As long as we understand each other.

Lionel Ooh-ar. That all then?

Ruth That is definitely all, Lionel, thank you.

Lionel (*miming pinching her bottom*) See yer then. (*He bolts towards the back door*)

Gerald enters, catches hold of Lionel and waltzes him round once before he exits

Gerald (*looking after him, in a black mood*) What the devil! What's the matter with him?

Ruth (*moving to look out of the front window*) How should I know; I found him here. He seems to come and go as he likes. You were quick. Is the car O.K.?

Gerald (*moving to the sofa and sitting*) Have to take it in to the garage tomorrow, but it's quite safe. We can run down to the *Red Lion* for dinner, if that's what's worrying you.

Ruth (*moving swiftly to the stairs door*) No, Gerald, I don't think I want to go anywhere with you tonight, I think I'll go to bed.

Gerald Do by all means. Away you go, don't mind me!

Ruth (*coming back*) Sleeping arrangements will be the same as last night. Well, almost, I mean you won't have Mr Day for company.

Gerald What's it matter to you who I have for company? Having kept me at arm's length all day, all you've got to do is to get yourself safely through the night.

Ruth (*moving swiftly back to the stair's door*) If you're going to start an argument, I'm going.

Gerald (*rising and rushing up to her*) Don't go, Ruth; I'm sorry, I'm an old bear. Please stay, if only for a little while. Let's stay friends at least.

Ruth (*looking at him for a moment and then smiling*) All right, friends it is – but not for long mind and no more of this afternoon's pranks, agreed?

Gerald Of course, you know me.

Ruth That's the trouble—I do.

Gerald (*steering her to the sofa and then moving up to the kitchen*) Go and sit down then and I'll get some drinks.

Ruth sits on the sofa, thinks better of it and moves to the armchair

Ruth Any of that whisky left that you mixed the Horlicks with?

Gerald Good idea, that's the spirit, darling. I'll join you. Want anything with it?

Ruth Water will do, if there is any.

Gerald There's a bucket here. (*Looking round*) Jug, jug—ah. (*He finds a jug and dips it in the bucket*) Glasses, glasses? We've only got wine glasses unless we use the Days' tumblers.

Ruth Any sort.
Gerald Right. Shan't be a moment.

Ruth lies back with her eyes closed. Gerald comes down from the kitchen to the fireplace and hands her a tumbler half full of whisky. He then sits on the sofa with his own drink

Eh, that's not very friendly, what's wrong with the sofa?
Ruth (*opening her eyes*) Heavens, that's not whisky, is it?
Gerald Mostly water. (*patting the seat next to him*) Come on, I won't bite. You promised to be nice to "G", remember.
Ruth (*moving to sit beside him*) Depends on your interpretation of nice. (*She takes a sip and coughs*) I thought you said it was mostly water.
Gerald Fire water, yes.
Ruth (*holding up her drink and looking at it*) I doubt if the Indians could have survived this.
Gerald Go on, it'll revive you; put a sparkle in your eye.
Ruth It's the sparkle in your eye, I'm worried about.

They sip their drinks in silence for a moment

Gerald (*turning to her and taking her hand*) Ruth, I'm not just a philanderer, you really are important to me. I could ...
Ruth What could you do?
Gerald Love you, fully, completely, utterly.
Ruth Occasionally.
Gerald Don't joke, Ruth. Can't you tell I'm serious?
Ruth (*pushing him away*) Don't, Gerald, please. You know perfectly well you're not.

They sip their drinks in silence again

Gerald (*turning to her again*) If you reject me, I'm finished – you know that.
Ruth There'll only be one way out, I know. Look, I must tell you why I came on this week-end. You see ...
Gerald (*taking her empty glass and putting his with it on the floor, then turning back to her and taking her in his arms*) There's no need for confessions, no need for guilt, just live out the here and now. (*He kisses her*)
Ruth Gerald, I feel ...
Gerald I know you do, my darling, I know.
Dora (*off*) Bolting like a startled rabbit, he were. I dunno what had got into him, do I?
Gerald Blast! (*He scrambles to his feet and crosses rapidly to the front window*)

Dora and Teresa enter through the back door

Teresa Didn't even look round when we shouted. Must have heard us.
Dora (*to Ruth*) You know what's up with Lionel?
Ruth Lionel? He was here but I don't know ...
Gerald Of course not, how would you expect Ruth to know anything about Lionel's doings.

Dora (*sitting at the table, rubbing her legs*) Lor, gal, proper done in I are and no mistake.

Teresa comes down from the kitchen, chewing an apple, and sits above the table

Teresa (*to Gerald*) How'd it go on "Devil's Bum" then? Did yer get what yer wanted?

Ruth No, he did not. And he's not too pleased about it either.

Dora Well, we oughter get ter bed, gal, we shall have ter do the milking tommorrow as yer dad's not coming home.

Teresa Too early ter go ter bed, Mum.

Gerald Oh, so Mr Day's not coming home then?

Dora Playing cricket again, ain't he? Silly old fool; they only takes him along for a laugh.

Gerald Is he staying the night, then?

Dora With his cousin, he says. (*Turning to Teresa*) You better come in with me again tonight, gal, so Miss Hill can have a proper night's rest for a change.

Ruth That's nice. Last night was a bit rough.

Teresa All right, Mum, but we don't have ter go yet, do we?

Ruth The hours before midnight are the ones that count, you know, Teresa.

Gerald Yes, if you want to keep that young figure and your beautiful, pink skin, you must have plenty of rest.

Teresa Ain't pink, it's brown.

Gerald But not all over, Teresa, surely?

Teresa (*jumping up*) Told yer he did, Mum! You're a dirty old man, that's what you are! (*She throws her apple at Gerald and then dashes upstairs, crying*)

Teresa exits

Gerald Now what have I done? I seem destined to upset every woman I meet.

Dora She thinks you put her nightie on last night.

Gerald She what?

Ruth Of course he didn't, as if I would let him. I put it on for her; made him stand on the landing.

Dora Guessed that's what happened. His sort are better at taking nighties off.

Gerald Well, you're quite safe!

Dora (*rising*) What's that?

Ruth It's all right, Mrs Day. He's just in a bad temper.

Gerald Yes, sorry, I'm a bit strung up.

Dora Oughter be, yer mean. (*She is struck by a spasm in her leg*) Ooh, come on, you old devils, yer won't be no better till I gets yer to bed. (*She hobbles across to the stair door, then turns to Ruth*) 'E'll be all right on the sofa ternight, being as Tom's away. Serve him right!

Dora exits, closing the stairs door behind her

Gerald (*sitting at the table*) That woman's getting on my nerves.

Ruth (*picking up the glasses and taking them up to the kitchen*) Well, I'm for joining them – this country air.

Gerald That's right, join the club, leave me down here on my own. Might as well end the day as miserably as it began.

Ruth (*from the kitchen*) You're certainly not much fun to be with in your present mood.

Gerald What do you expect, the way you've treated me.

Ruth (*returning*) That's the trouble, isn't it: I haven't treated you at all.

Gerald I hate to say this, Ruth, but you're a prude.

Ruth Is that what you call someone who doesn't strip off on the top of a hill?

Gerald There wasn't a soul about for miles, nothing but rabbits.

Ruth (*moving to the stairs door*) I didn't like the way they stared at me with those great brown eyes. (*Turning to him*) Besides, some of them might have been bucks.

Gerald (*moving quickly to her*) I'm not letting you go! You promised. It's not yet nine o'clock; I'll never get to sleep on that sofa. You just can't leave me to hours of sleepless hell! Ruth, be fair!

Ruth It's been a long day, Gerald.

Gerald It'll be a longer night if you go now.

Ruth Please don't press me to. I came here with a firm resolve, but you're so persistent. You quite exhaust me.

Gerald (*drawing her back to the sofa*) The last thing I want to do is exhaust you but you mustn't make me feel as if I'm nothing but a sex fiend with only one thought in my mind. (*He manœuvres her on to the sofa*) That's very naughty of you, Ruth.

Ruth Can you blame me if I think that?

Gerald (*sitting beside her*) You don't understand men, do you? You're misinterpreting my intentions because you've been conditioned to think that all men are beasts. Your mother certainly has a lot to answer for.

Ruth I'm not all innocence, you know: I have been out in the world for a few years. I won't deny that I would like you to possess me, but——

Gerald Then please let me—please.

Ruth —but you won't because of Alison.

Gerald She wouldn't be the loser; my passion is inexhaustible. I have just too much love for one women. You're the only other in my life. If I had you both, I should be complete.

Ruth Gerald, just what am I to do with you?

Gerald (*taking her in his arms*) Love me, love me.

Ruth (*pushing him away, jumping to her feet*) No, no, Gerald! If you won't think of Alison, I must!

Gerald Ruth, please!

Ruth (*moving swiftly to the stairs door*) No, Gerald!

Gerald (*rising and rushing up to her*) I swear Alison will not be hurt. Ruth, how can you be so cruel!

Ruth I'm being cruel out of my great affection for you, Gerald. Good night!

Gerald (*grabbing her*) Right! You've asked for this and you're going to get

it! (*He throws her from him, then advances on her slowly*) Come here!
(*Bending his arm*) Feel this! (*He searches desperately for his muscle*)

Ruth What?

Gerald (*taking hold of her and pulling her close*) Come here! (*He pushes her
away to arm's length*) Now! Look me straight between the eyes—I mean—
thighs!

Ruth What?

Gerald pulls her close to him and breathes hard on her neck

What the hell are you doing?

Gerald (*pulling her head back by her hair*) O.K., kid, quit struggling, there
ain't no going back now! Take what's coming to yer! (*He throws her on to
the sofa, moves away "paws" the ground with his feet and charges across to
dive on her*)

Ruth Gerald, stop clowning!

He pulls up short, as he was launching himself upon her

Gerald Clowning?

Ruth You weren't serious? Holy Moses, I think you were! (*She bursts into
peals of laughter, then mimics him*) Look me straight between the thighs!
Really, Gerald.

Gerald (*clutching his chest*) My God! (*He staggers away and leans on the
table*)

Ruth (*rising*) What on earth? (*Going to him*) Gerald, what's wrong, for
Heaven's sake, what is it? Stop fooling!

Gerald (*staggering below her to the sofa*) Ah—ah—ah—ah, a seizure.

Ruth (*rushing to him, kneeling*) You're joking, please tell me you're joking.

Gerald (*weakly*) Doctor warned me; I didn't listen.

Ruth Doctor? What did he say?

Gerald Said it would happen this way.

Ruth (*sitting beside him and putting her arm round him*) Gerald, darling.

Gerald Hold me, Ruth, hold me tight.

*Gerald groans, and his groan is immediately followed by a groan from Debbie
who, if the inset bedroom is used, gets out of bed and disappears from sight*

Ruth My poor, poor darling, you really are suffering.

Gerald groans; Debbie groans

The whole house echoes with your pain.

Gerald groans; Debbie groans. Then she comes lumping down the stairs

Gerald (*jumping up and moving to the fireplace*) Blast! I'll wring that bloody
woman's neck for this!

Ruth (*jumping up and attacking him*) Gerald, you absolute beast! How could
you?

The stairs door opens and Debbie staggers in, moaning

Gerald Good Heavens, it's Debbie! What on earth's the matter with her?

Ruth (*moving to Debbie*) She's about to give birth, that's what.
Gerald She can't, not here!
Ruth You tell her that.
Gerald (*rushing up to Debbie*) Now, Debbie, don't be a silly girl, don't do anything you'll regret.
Ruth Stop twittering and help me get her to the sofa!

They help the moaning Debbie to the sofa. As they do so, the Land Rover screeches to a halt outside

   A terrified Lionel bursts through the front door

Lionel (*rushing in*) I got it, I got it, Deb. (*He takes in the scene*) Oh, hell!
Gerald Lionel! Just the man. Get her to the hospital, quick!
Ruth (*kneeling by Debbie*) She'll never make it.
Gerald Then what? I can't help her: I faint if I cut my finger.
Ruth (*rising*) Pull yourself together, Gerald. Go and find some clean towels! Lionel, put the kettle on, we're going to need lashings of hot water.
Lionel What fer? You going to give her a bath?

Gerald rushes up to the kitchen area

Ruth Oh, and find a sharp knife.
Gerald (*stopping*) Knife? You're not going to ...?
Ruth To cut the cord, silly.
Gerald (*almost fainting*) Cord! Oh, my God!
Lionel (*panicking and running out of the front door, leaving it open*) Mum! Mum!

   Lionel exits

Ruth (*moving to close door then returning*) Men! Come here, Gerald, and comfort Debbie; I'll see to it.
Gerald (*coming slowly to Ruth*) It's not my fault; I never could stand anything biological.
Ruth Really. (*Steering him to the sofa and pushing him down on his knees beside Debbie*) Well, just talk to her, boost her confidence. (*Moving up to the stairs door*) I'll find a towel.

   Ruth exits up to the stairs door

Gerald (*putting his arm round Debbie*) Now, don't you worry, Debbie. Big "G" is here. That's right, grip big "G's' hand, he'll see you through.

The front door opens quietly and Alison appears. She turns and closes the door so that she does not see Gerald and Debbie

Alison Yoo, hoo, darling, surprise, surpri ... (*Her voice trails away as she takes in the scene*)
Gerald (*weakly*) Alison!
Alison (*recovering*) Just thought I'd surprise you – evidently I have.
Gerald (*rising*) Now, now, darling, don't go jumping to any silly conclusions.
Debbie groans

Alison Good Lord, she's about to ... (*Putting down her bag on the table and moving above the sofa*) It's all right, love, I'm here now. (*She picks up Debbie's hand and feels her pulse*) Yes, it won't be long now—just relax. (*To Gerald*) By heck, lad, you've got some explaining to do.

Gerald She's nothing to do with me.

Alison No,? Well, perhaps you can explain what she's doing here in your cottage, rented for the week-end?

Gerald I don't know, she just appeared.

Alison Just appeared, did she? A pretty substantial materialization, wouldn't you say?

Ruth emerges from the stairs door

Ruth Thank goodness I packed a spare ... Alison!

Alison Ruth!

Gerald You know each other?

Alison What on earth are you doing here? (*She looks from one to the other*) I see – Ruth, how could you? I thought you were my best friend.

Gerald Your friend?

Alison And what about you, Ruth, did you just appear?

Gerald You've got it all wrong, darling: you're the only one, the only one.

Teresa appears from the stairs door, dressed in her nightie

Teresa What's all the noise?

Alison The only one, am I?

Gerald Good Lord, you don't think ...?

Dora, also dressed in her nightie, emerges from the stairs door

Dora What's going on? 'Nough ter wake the dead.

Alison They come in all sizes!

Debbie gives an enormous groan

Never mind, it'll wait; this won't.

Dora What the hell! Debbie? She ain't going ter ...?

Alison (*crisply*) Oh, yes she is. (*Moving to the table to get her bag*) Hand on deck everybody—boiling water, towels!

Gerald and Ruth rush to the kitchen

Dora (*pushing Teresa up the stairs*) 'Ere, gal, you get up them stairs!

CURTAIN

After the Curtain falls there is the sound of two sharp slaps, followed by the cry of a baby

SCENE 3

The same. Two hours later

When the Curtain rises, the lamp is lit. Dora is sitting at the table, nursing the baby. Teresa is sitting in the armchair. A tight-lipped Alison is up in the kitchen area washing at the sink. Debbie is still on the sofa, but now propped up with cushions. Gerald is standing by the fireplace and Ruth sits at the table. Dora is pulling faces at the baby.

Dora Who's a lovely, little old gal, den? Ooh, what a big smile for Auntie Dora. Does she like Aunty's face den, does she?

Teresa She's got wind, Mum. That's what makes them smile, told us that at school.

Gerald (*to Debbie*) Feeling better now?

Debbie Not too bad, a bit wobbly.

Alison (*sweeping down from the kitchen*) Let the girl rest! She doesn't want any of your chat. (*Ruffling Debbie's hair as she passes above sofa*) Do you, love? Had enough trouble from his sort, I should think. (*Looking round*) I think I've cleared everything.

Gerald (*moving to the chair above the table, inviting Alison to sit on it*) You were wonderful, darling, but come and sit down and have a little rest.

Alison (*ignoring him*) Yes, I think that's everything.

Gerald (*to Alison*) You could use a drink, I expect?

Alison gives him an icy look and sweeps back up into the kitchen

(*To Ruth*) Stand by for blasting.

Ruth Don't joke, Gerald, I feel terrible. What must she think of me?

Lily (*off*) No, you don't, me boy, you're going ter look that gal in the face!

The front door bursts open and Lily Flack drags Lionel in by his short hair

Lionel Leave off, Mum! (*He manages to escape Lily's grasp as she turns to close the door*)

Lily (*closing the door*) Here we are, gal, found him hiding in the barn. (*Crossing to the sofa.*) His dad's gone for the doctor. (*Realizing that Debbie is no longer pregnant*) Ooh-er!

Dora (*holding up the baby*) This what yer looking for, gal?

Lionel goes to Dora to peer at the baby

Lily (*turning and seeing the baby*) What? Oh, my goodness! (*Turning to Lionel*) Now look what you've been and gone and done! (*She cuffs his ear*)

Lionel Ow!

Teresa (*jumping up and slapping Lionel's face, then returning to her seat*) And there's one from me!

Debbie Give him one for me, Teresa.

Teresa jumps up again, takes another swing at Lionel, misses and nearly catches Lily. She then returns to her chair

Lionel (*in anticipation*) Ow!

Lily (*catching hold of Lionel by his short hair and forcing him on his knees beside the sofa*) Now, you just tell Debbie you're sorry. Go on now! (*She leaves him and turns to take the baby from Dora*)

Lionel I are sorry, Deb, honest, only I were frit.

Gerald moves to the fireplace

Debbie 'S all right, Lionel, I were frit an' all. You do like me, Lionel?
Lionel (*sitting on the sofa with Debbie*) Yeah, 'course I do, Deb.
Debbie And our little old gal?

Lily holds the baby for Lionel to see

Lionel (*looking round coyly at the baby*) Ooh-ah, bit of all right she are.
Lily Is an' all. (*She goes to show the baby to Ruth.*) Ain't she a little love?

The front door opens and Flack appears

Flack The doctor says he won't be long. (*Taking in the scene*) Ah—up, well
I'd go to—she's had it then and I run all the way to the phone. Damn me,
then! (*Seeing Lionel*) And you, you young bugger . . . (*To Debbie*) Asked yer to
marry him yet, has he?
Lionel (*looking up at his father*) Who, me, Dad?
Debbie Not yet, Mr Flack, but he were just going to, wan't you, Lionel?
Flack I bloody hope he were! (*Picking up Lionel by the scruff of his neck and
dumping him on his knees in front of Debbie*) Go on, then, get on with it!
Lionel Dunno what ter say.
Gerald How about: O.K., kid, quit struggling, there ain't no going back
now.

Lionel gives him a poisonous look

Lily Funny sort of proposal that are. I'd give him a kick in the . . .
Flack He'll feel my boot if he don't get on with it!
Lionel How about it then, Deb, shall us get hitched?
Gerald Beautifully put, don't you think so, Ruth?
Ruth Yes, Lionel's approach is very direct, isn't it, Lionel?
Lionel (*starting to rise and turning to Ruth*) Ooh-ar.
Flack (*pushing him down again*) That's all right, then. Now . . .
Teresa She ain't said yes, yet. I wouldn't have him at any price.
Dora That's a relief, anyhow.
Lily And what might yer mean by that, Dora Day?
Flack (*to Lily*) Stop yer gabbin', woman. Now, gal, fancy me for yer dad-in-
law do yer?
Lily That'll put her off for sure.
Flack Hold yer tongue, woman. Well, Deb, what about it? Do yer want me,
I mean him?
Debbie I suppose I do, Ain't got a lot of choice really, have I?
Dora Make lovely pair, don't they.
Lily (*handing the baby to Dora*) Well, that's settled then and ain't it lucky,
Dora, that you're a-moving; they'll be able to have this here little old
cottage, seeing as you're leaving it.
Flack (*moving to Lily*) Here, hold on, woman, what about me rent?
Lily Rent! I hopes, Bill Flack, as how you'll a give it to them as a wedding
present.
Flack You what? Ain't made a money, woman!
Lily (*pointing to the baby*) You ain't even looked at yer granddaughter yet.
(*Pointing to the baby*) Go on, look at her! Little love, ain't she?

Flack (*leaning forward and lifting the shawl round its face with his pipe*) Bit red, ain't it?

Lily Bit red! Is that all you can say, your first grandchild, a bit red! Be of more interest if you could take her down the market and sell her fer a few pounds, wouldn't she? Well you listen ter me, Bill Flack, I've had a basin full of your meanness I have ...

Flack Give over, woman, I'll ...

Lily (*with hands on hips*) You're giving them this cottage whether you likes it or not - I've been your bloomin' doormat long enough! Now, you and Lionel carry our Deb out ter the Land Rover and while she's having a few days' rest at the farm, you and him can give this here cottage a bit of a smartening up. Go on now!

Flack (*muttering under his breath, and moving to the sofa*) Come on, boy, grab hold on her. You take the top end. Teresa, open the door, there's a good old gal.

Lionel rises and moves to pick up Debbie by the shoulders. Flack takes her feet. Teresa opens the front door

Debbie (*as Flack and Lionel attempt to lift her*) Wait a bit, I want ter thank "G's" wife, I do.

Lionel (*dropping Debbie back on to the sofa*) Ooh-ah, "G's" wife, who's she then?

Flack drops Debbie's feet and attempts to cuff Lionel

Ruth (*shouting to Alison in the kitchen*) Alison, Debbie wants to thank you.

Alison (*coming down to the sofa*) I heard.

Gerald Last summer I helped her with the milking - she used to call me Uncle "G"!

Dora "Uncle," that's a good'un, that is!

Debbie We was just friends, that's all. You got a dirty mind you have, Dora Day.

Dora P'raps I have, gal, p'raps I have. Ain't ter be wondered at with the goin's on round here.

Alison Never mind, Debbie. (*With a look at Gerald*) I know you're not to blame.

Teresa (*still holding the front door open*) Come on then, ain't a bloomin' doorstop, yer know.

Flack and Lionel pick up Debbie again

Alison Have a good rest, love, and you'll be fine. Look after her now, Lionel.

Lionel Ooh-ah.

They lift her off the sofa by swinging her together

Flack Two, three—erp.

Lily Go easy, you great gorms, she ain't a bale of hay!

Lionel and Flack carry Debbie out. Teresa follows, to see them off

Debbie (*as they go*) Thanks, Mrs Turner, you was lovely. 'Bye all.

Lily (*following them out*) Watch what you're doing, man! I'll sort yer out from now on, Bill Flack. You can buy some new fencing for that old bull of yourn and it's about time yer paid old Tom a decent wage. (*Turning at the door to Dora*) How yer expect her ter manage, I don't know. Don't you worry, gal, I'll see Tom gets what's coming to him.

Dora He don't know what's coming to him yet, gal. 'Bout time we sorted them buggers out.

Lily goes out

Lily (*shouting after Flack as she goes*) Go on you two! What yer 'anging 'bout fer? Git in the Land Rover!

As soon as Lily disappears, Lionel comes back, looks around, scratching his head, then remembers what he has come back for. He takes the baby from Dora, holds it up to his face, smiles at it and then, tucking it under one arm, exits through the front door, closing it after him

Alison Poor, little Debbie, fancy being tied to an oaf like Lionel. Still it seems that some women can't resist that sort, more fools them. Don't you think so, Ruth?

Ruth Well, I ...

Alison 'Course you do—(*looking at Gerald*)—you like the flabby, uncle type, don't you?

Gerald Alison!

Alison I'll talk to you later, Uncle "G". (*She sweeps off to the kitchen*)

The Land Rover starts up and departs

Dora (*rubbing her legs*) Forgot all about you, you old buggers, what with the baby and everything. Suppose you'll give me no peace till I gets yer ter bed.

Teresa returns

Teresa (*closing the door and leaning against it*) I can cross Lionel off my list, he's had it now.

Dora Had it a long time ago, gal, that's for sure. You've had a lucky escape there, I can tell yer. (*Struggling to her feet and limping up to the stairs door*) Well, come on, gal, we got the milking ter do termorrer, remember. (*Turning to speak to Gerald and Ruth*) Can't think how you're all going ter sleep. Still, I reckons that won't bother you lot much ternight. (*To Gerald*) I reckons as how you'll finish up on "Devil's Bum", mate.

Dora disappears up the stairs, closing the door after her

Gerald Beats me what a sensible girl like you, Teresa, saw in Lionel.

Teresa He din't half kiss nice.

Ruth Yes, he did, didn't he?

Gerald What?

Ruth (*quickly*) From what I saw, him and Teresa, I mean.

Gerald Ah.

Teresa (*going to the stairs door*) Well, good night, then.
Ruth Good night, Teresa, you'll soon forget about Lionel. It won't be too
   hard.

Teresa bursts into tears and exits up the stairs, closing the door after her

Gerald Well, if I didn't know you, I should have said you fancied Lionel.
Ruth Just as well you know me then, isn't it?
Alison (*calling from the kitchen*) All gone to bed, have they?
Gerald (*calling to her*) Yes, darling, just this minute. (*To Ruth*) Here comes
   the inquisition.
Alison (*coming down to Gerald*) What was that, Gerald?
Gerald Intuition, dear, I said intuition told you the coast was clear.
Alison Yes, Gerald, it's inquisition time. So, who's going to start?
Gerald Alison, I know things look bad.
Alison Positively rotten, Gerald.
Ruth But it's not what you think, really it's not.
Alison (*sitting at the table*) No, of course, I'm being silly, aren't I? Every-
   thing's just as I expected: I come down here, find him holding a strange
   girl's hand and my best friend skulking upstairs to say nothing of . . .
Ruth I was not skulking. (*Sitting*) Anyway, you know all about Debbie
   now; know that wasn't what you thought.
Alison And I'm only half convinced on that.
Gerald (*shocked*) Alison!
Alison Half convinced, Uncle "G", but I am trying to think of a convincing
   reason why my friend should be shacked up with my husband in a remote
   country cottage.
Gerald (*sitting on the sofa*) Shacked up! I like that!
Alison And do you know, hard as it is to believe, I haven't come up with a
   single, plausible explanation. Now, Gerald, darling, perhaps you'd like to
   start.

The front door opens and Flack returns

Flack They gone off all right. Missus sent me back ter ask if yer staying
   tomorrer night. If you ain't, I gotter start the decorating.
Gerald (*rising, going to Flack and taking him up to the kitchen*) Ah, Flack,
   old chap, I'm glad you popped back. I'd like to wet the baby's head. Have
   a drink with me.

Alison marches determinedly to the front door and stands holding it open

Flack Well, don't mind if I do.
Alison We won't be staying tonight, and I'm sure Mr Flack's got more
   important things to do.
Flack (*stopping, turning and making a dejected exit through the front
   door*) Reckon you're right, Missus, gotter get after Hamish. Be off then.
   You'd better give the key ter Dora. I ain't allowed keys no more.

   Flack goes out

Alison closes the door and returns to her seat
Alison I'm waiting, Gerald.

Gerald (*moving down to her*) Are you, darling. Now, what were we saying, old Flack's put it right out of my mind.

Alison He hasn't out of mine. You were about to explain how you and Ruth happened to be in this cottage together, remember?

Gerald (*moving below the sofa*) Ah, yes, it's coming back to me.

Alison Good, so let's hear it!

Gerald (*sitting on the sofa*) I – I think Ruth should put her side first.

Alison Ladies first, of course, you were always the perfect gentleman, Gerald.

Ruth (*rising*) I think it might be best if I spoke first, Alison. I hope this won't hurt you too much, Gerald.

Gerald Me? I've nothing to hide.

Alison Goody for you. (*To Ruth*) Well?

Ruth I know I've been stupid but I did it for you, Alison, really I did.

Alison For me? How nice, but I don't see ...

Ruth When we had that long chat a few weeks ago after meeting up again and you told me how worried you were about Gerald losing interest and playing around with other women.

Gerald Me? Playing around!

Ruth Well, I made it my business to keep an eye on him when he came into the library.

Alison And what did you find?

Ruth Silly flirting, that's all, like most middle-aged men.

Gerald Middle-aged?

Alison Middle-aged!

Ruth There seemed to be nothing more in it than that. But for your peace of mind, Alison, I felt I had better make sure. After all, third-hand information is never conclusive is it?

Alison So you tried a bit of first-hand?

Ruth In a way, yes: I pretended to be taken with him.

Gerald (*half rising*) Pretended! My God, I'll never trust another woman!

Alison Gerald! (*To Ruth*) Yes?

Gerald sinks back on to the sofa

Ruth Well, he took me out to lunch a few times. Made a few suggestions, just sexy talk, you know.

Alison Haven't experienced it lately, but go on.

Ruth So, having chatted him up and got him to show off his feathers, I said to myself, "Right, cock, now let's see what you're really made of".

Alison I see; you got him to put his money where his beak is, so to speak.

Ruth Yes, something like that.

Alison Don't stop – please go on.

Ruth (*moving below the table*) Well, it was a risk of course.

Alison Enormous!

Gerald Not all that enormous, darling.

Alison Quiet you!

Ruth Anyway, I made up my mind to take the risk, Alison, for your sake.

Alison (*standing*) Sweet of you. (*Moving between Ruth and Gerald*) So you planned to spend this week-end with Gerald in the hope that he would expose himself—if you'll excuse the expression.

Ruth Yes, loosely speaking.

Alison Well? (*Pause*) Well, did he? I mean what have I got: a rampant old bull or a woolly old sheep in cock's feathers? Did he bleat or did he crow?

Gerald flaps his elbows in imitation of a rooster as a signal to Ruth. Alison turns and catches him. He turns it into a yawn

Tired dear?

Gerald Yes, it's been an exhausting week-end.

Alison Really?

Gerald (*quickly*) I mean – we've had very little sleep.

Alison I see.

Gerald No, the Days, Flack, the bull they ...

Alison Well, well. (*She looks at Ruth*) I'm waiting, Ruth, for your prognosis.

Ruth I assure you he's got nothing to crow about. (*Moving round to sit in the chair above the table*) He's absolutely harmless; he couldn't be unfaithful to you if he was locked in a harem for the night.

Gerald Steady on now, Ruth.

Alison (*crossing below the sofa and turning to look down on Gerald*) I don't know whether I should be reassured by that or not.

Gerald (*rising*) I ought to be hopping mad with both of you. With you, Alison, for doubting me—(*moving towards Ruth*)—and with you, Ruth, for deliberately testing me out. Whatever gave you the idea that I would fall for your little seduction routine, beats me. As far as I was concerned, I only invited you because you write shorthand.

Alison Yes, my lad—well, remind me next week to buy you a tape recorder. But right now, you can do penance by taking us both out to dinner. (*Holding out her hand*) My coat, please!

Gerald (*moving swiftly to the table, picking up Alison's coat from the chair, and returning to help her on with it*) What a good idea, I can't wait to leave this grotty cottage.

Ruth What, this little rural heaven, haven of peace and tranquillity?

Gerald My foot! Come on, let's pack up and go. We'll eat at the *Red Lion* and then go straight back to town. (*Going up to the stairs door*) I'll get the cases. Have you left anything unpacked, Ruth?

Ruth (*rising and going into the kitchen*) Only my nightie on the small bed. For God's sake, don't wake the Days though.

Gerald goes up the stairs and, if the inset bedroom is used, appears in the bedroom. He collects Ruth's case and disappears from view

Alison Is there anything else?

Ruth Only this case of wine, I'll bring it. (*She returns from the kitchen carrying the wine which she places on the table*)

Alison Was that your idea, too?

Ruth What?

Alison The wine – the acid test as it were.

Ruth (*laughing*) No, he bought that locally. Thinks he got a real bargain.

Gerald reappears with two cases

Gerald (*moving to the front door*) We'll leave that for the Days as a little thank you present. They're partial to that old cider.
Ruth Well, young Teresa is, or certainly was. We'd better leave them a note then. (*Looking round*) If I can find anything to write on.

Gerald feels in his inside pocket and produces the notes that he wrote as a leg-pull on Lionel

Alison (*moving to the fireplace and picking up the note that Ruth left for Gerald*) Here, will this do? It doesn't appear to be wanted. (*She stares at it*)
Gerald (*handing his notes to Ruth*) Here, use this, it's only scrap.

Ruth takes the notes and hunts in her bag for a pen

Alison Gerald, this is a note addressed to you.
Gerald Me?
Alison If you answer to "Big G", yes (*Tearing it open*) Shall I read it to you?
Ruth (*rising and making a move towards her*) No, Alison, please!
Alison (*reading*) "My poor big G, sorry to disappoint you, but I'm quite worn out trying to fend you off. You won't be alone though, you'll have someone to cuddle up to. Ruth."

Ruth sits above the table

Fending off, eh?
Gerald (*quickly*) From work, Alison. I was simply working her too hard at the earthwork. (*To Ruth*) What a brute I am, my dear, I didn't realize.
Ruth He has such a capacity – for work.
Alison And who did he cuddle up to, Teresa?
Ruth No, no, Mr Day turned up drunk and collapsed on the sofa – it was a joke.
Alison I hope it was or Gerald's changed his inclinations. (*Putting the note on the table and picking up the notes that Gerald had given to Ruth*) Well, exhibit "A" seems to support your motive, Ruth, but casts doubt on your judgement. What's that you've got there, exhibit "B"? Do let me see. (*Reading*) "Take the strong man approach: look her straight between the thighs; grab her to you; let her feel your muscles." (*Looking up*) What on earth is this?
Ruth (*rising and laughing*) Of course! Lionel! You've been taking lessons from Lionel.
Gerald It was only a joke – just a minute, how do you know it was Lionel?
Ruth (*stopping laughing and escaping to the fireplace*) Never mind. What else is there, Alison?
Alison (*reading*) "Breathe on back of neck, get her panting." (*Looking up*) I don't believe this.
Ruth I do, go on.
Alison (*reading*) "Say; O.K. kid, quit struggling, it won't do yer no good. Just take what's coming to you."

Ruth (*laughing hysterically and collapsing on the sofa*) "Take what's coming to yer", oh, no.

Alison (*laughing hysterically and collapsing on the arm on the sofa*) "Won't do yer no good". (*Pointing at Gerald*) Not with him, it wouldn't!

Gerald Very funny! Go on, laugh your silly heads off! Would you like me to slip on a banana skin, blow smoke out of my ears, put my face in a custard tart? (*He sits on a chair at the table and sulks*)

Alison (*recovering*) No, my lad, you're quite right, it's not funny at all. (*Rising*) What you can do is find your own way home. Ruth and I will have a meal on our own. (*Marching down to the front door*) Come on, Ruth, let's leave him. (*Turning to Gerald*) And I might not be home for a few days. It'll give you time to appreciate me.

Ruth (*rising, moving above the table and giving an exaggerated nudge to Gerald as she passes him*) So long kid, keep flexing those muscles.

Laughing, both Ruth and Alison exit through the front door. There is the roar of a bull and, terrified, they both rush back, slam the door shut and rush to Gerald

It's Hamish!

Alison Don't just sit there, Gerald, do something!

Gerald (*rising with the two girls clinging to him*) Me? What can little weak me do?

Alison Drive him off! Please!

Gerald I'd be no match for him.

Ruth Yes, you would. We were only joking, you know that.

Alison We weren't laughing at you.

Ruth As if you needed notes.

Alison Of course, he doesn't. Darling, please get rid of that bull!

Gerald You'll promise to come home tonight if I do?

Alison Yes, of course I will.

Gerald And never laugh at me again, even in bed?

Alison Never, I promise.

Gerald Ruth?

Alison (*outraged*) Gerald!

Ruth No, never anywhere, my Tarzan.

Gerald (*pushing them behind him*) Right, stand back, girls! Let the brute meet his master! (*Gerald expands his chest and flexes his muscles then marches towards the door*) Good boy, Hamish, come along now, big "G" wants you!

As Gerald reaches the door, there is the mighty roar of a bull and its two horns smash through. Gerald staggers back, and the two women, pointing at the horns, cling to each other, screaming, as—

CURTAIN *falls*

FURNITURE AND PROPERTY LIST

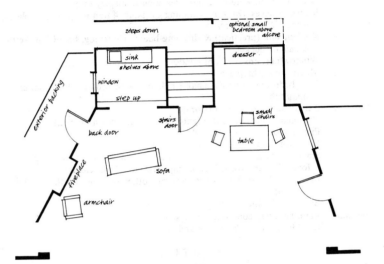

Optional small bedroom

ACT I

Scene 1

On stage:	Sofa. *On it:* cushions
	Armchair
	3 kitchen chairs
	Table
	Dresser. *On it:* a number of plates & cups, display only
	Kitchen shelves. *On them:* camping gas lamp, 4 tumbler glasses, 4 plates, teapot, 2 mugs, torch
	Kitchen sink (practical) & draining-board. *On it:* jug, bread bin, kettle. *Beside it:* bucket
	Window curtains on front window & in bedroom (if used)
	Mirror above fireplace
	Inset bedroom (if used): small single bed with bedding, bedroom chair, small table
Off stage:	2 small suitcases, parcel (**Dora**)
	Old, small suitcase. *In it:* nightdress, dressing-gown (**Teresa**)
	Pile of sheets & blankets (**Lily**)
	New large suitcase, small suitcase (**Ruth**)
	Small cardboard box. *In it:* insulated food box, 2 wine glasses, 2 knives, 2 forks, 2 soup bowls, 2 table napkins, tablecloth (**Gerald**)
	Large cardboard box. *In it:* several bottles of wine, bottle of whisky (**Gerald**)
	Basket with pint of milk, eggs (**Debbie**)
Personal:	**Ruth:** handbag containing notepaper, pen
	Gerald: pocket corkscrew, matches

ACT II

Scene 1

Strike:	Lamp back to kitchen
Set:	Bed made
	On table: remains of breakfast—4 cups, 4 knives, marmalade, butter, half loaf of bread on bread-board, bread knife. (Note: 3 place settings should have been used)
	On kitchen draining-board: 4 clean cups, 4 saucers, teapot containing tea, bottle of milk
Personal:	**Dora:** shopping bag
	Lily: basket of vegetables
	Gerald: notepaper, pencil

Scene 2

Set:	*In kitchen:* opened bottle of wine, bottle of whisky, 2 wine glasses, 2 tumblers, bucket of water, jug, apple
Personal:	**Alison:** bag

Scene 3

Set:	Lamp on table, alight
Check:	**Ruth's** case under bed in inset bedroom
Off stage:	Bull's horns (**Stage management**)

Gerald's suitcase
Ruth's suitcase (if inset bedroom not used)
Personal: **Dora:** baby doll, shawl
Gerald: notes

LIGHTING PLOT

Property fittings required: camping gas lamp
Interior. A cottage living-room, kitchen, stairs and bedroom (optional)
The same scene throughout

ACT I Scene 1   Evening

To open:	General effect of evening light. No light on bedroom	
Cue 1	**Teresa:** "Night, Lionel" *Bring up light in bedroom*	(Page 15)
Cue 2	**Dora** pulls **Teresa** from bedroom *Fade bedroom light*	(Page 15)

ACT I Scene 2   Evening

To open:	Effect of dusk	
Cue 3	As CURTAIN rises *Headlights flash across window*	(Page 16)
Cue 4	**Gerald** lights lamp *Bring up interior lighting on main set, with spot to indicate lamp source*	(Page 17)
Cue 5	**Ruth** mounts stairs *Bring up light in bedroom*	(Page 18)
Cue 6	**Gerald:** "I'll douse the light, then" *Dim main lights*	(Page 19)
Cue 7	As **Gerald** descends stairs *Fade bedroom light*	(Page 19)
Cue 8	**Teresa** turns up lamp *Bring up main set lighting as before*	(Page 19)
Cue 9	**Ruth** turns down lamp a little *Slight fade of general lighting*	(Page 22)
Cue 10	**Gerald** kisses **Ruth** *Headlights flash across window*	(Page 23)
Cue 11	**Dora** turns up lamp to full *Restore full lighting*	(Page 25)
Cue 12	**Dora:** "... he would if it suited." *Headlights flash across window*	(Page 25)
Cue 13	**Ruth** and **Gerald** carry **Teresa** upstairs *Bring up bedroom light*	(Page 30)
Cue 14	**Ruth** and **Gerald** leave bedroom *Fade bedroom light*	(Page 30)
Cue 15	**Lionel** appears in bedroom *Bring up bedroom light*	(Page 30)

Cue 16	**Teresa** runs from bedroom *Fade bedroom light*	(Page 30)
Cue 17	**Ruth** puts note on mantelpiece *Bring up bedroom light*	(Page 31)
Cue 18	**Lionel:** "... and take what's comin'. to yer!" *Fade bedroom light*	(Page 31)
Cue 19	**Gerald** turns out lamp *Total* BLACK-OUT	(Page 32)

ACT II Scene 1   Morning

To open	All lighting up to full daylight, except bedroom	
Cue 20	**Lionel:** "Get orf, you stupid git!" BLACK-OUT	(Page 42)

ACT II Scene 2   Evening

To open:	General effect of sunset. No light on bedroom	
Cue 21	As **Lionel** and **Debbie** mount stairs *Bring up bedroom light*	(Page 44)
Cue 22	As **Lionel** leaves bedroom *Fade bedroom light*	(Page 44)
Cue 23	**Gerald** groans *Bring up bedroom light*	(Page 49)
Cue 24	**Debbie** leaves bedroom *Fade bedroom light*	(Page 49)
Cue 25	**Dora:** "... you get up them stairs" *Quick* BLACK-OUT	(Page 51)

ACT II Scene 3   Night

To open:	Lamp lit. Interior lighting full up, except bedroom	
Cue 26	**Alison:** "I'll talk to you later, Uncle 'G'" *Headlights flash across window*	(Page 55)
Cue 27	As bull horns come through door *Fade all lighting except on front door*	(Page 60)

EFFECTS PLOT

ACT I

Scene 1

Cue 1	**Lily:** "... blowed as an old sheep in clover, I are." *Land Rover starts up and fades away*	(Page 2)
Cue 2	**Lily:** "... going ter let it was she?" *Car draws up and stops*	(Page 2)
Cue 3	**Gerald:** "... good for the appetite." *Bull bellow*	(Page 5)
Cue 4	**Flack:** "... if I catch yer!" *Bull bellow, further off*	(Page 5)
Cue 5	**Lionel:** "... a job lot down the market." *Car starts up and drives away*	(Page 13)

Scene 2

Cue 6	As CURTAIN rises *Car arrives and stops, doors slam*	(Page 16)
Cue 7	**Gerald:** "... a big thank-you kiss" *Bull bellow*	(Page 16)
Cue 8	**Gerald** kisses **Ruth** *Roar of tractor approaching and stopping*	(Page 23)
Cue 9	**Dora:** "... ring through his nose, he did" *Car starts up and drives away: followed by harvester*	(Page 25)

ACT II

Scene 1

Cue 10	**Lily:** "... too mean to drink much" *Bull bellow in distance*	(Page 39)

Scene 2

Cue 11	As CURTAIN rises *Loud bull bellow, twice*	(Page 43)
Cue 12	**Lionel:** "He's going ter charge, he are!" *Loud bull bellow*	(Page 43)
Cue 13	**Lionel** dashes in and slams door *Bull bellow, slightly further off*	(Page 43)
Cue 14	**Ruth** and **Gerald** help **Debbie** to sofa *Land Rover drives up and screeches to a halt*	(Page 50)
Cue 15	After CURTAIN falls *Two sharp slaps, followed by cry of baby*	(Page 51)

Scene 3

Cue 16	**Alison:** "I'll talk to you later, Uncle 'G'"	(Page 55)
	Land Rover starts up and drives away	
Cue 17	**Ruth** and **Alison** exit	(Page 60)
	Bull bellow, short distance away	
Cue 18	**Gerald:** "... big 'G' wants you" (*He reaches front door*)	(Page 60)
	Loud bull bellow	

Printed and bound in Great Britain by Butler & Tanner Ltd, Frome and London